THE GAME OF DATING

"THE LOST ART OF COURTSHIP"

DEDRICK R. BRIGGS

THE GAME OF DATING
THE LOST ART OF COURTSHIP

This book was printed in the United States of America.

All the stories related in this book are true, but most of the names have been changed to protect the privacy of the people mentioned.

ISBN:
Hardcover 978-1479756469
Softcover 978-0615755243

For additional information about this book, contact:

THE DEDRICK BRIGGS COMPANY
www.dedrickbriggs.com
info@dedrickbriggs.com

ACKNOWLEDGMENTS

This book is dedicated to my family, supporters and you the reader. I thank everyone for your hard work, dedication and the time you've given toward this project, I love you dearly.

For the development and production of the book, I feel a deep sense of gratitude:

— to my wife LaToya for devoting your time. We spent countless hours trying to make sure this was an excellent production. I love being married to you, your value is immeasurable.

— to my mother, I believe I am a visionary because you are.

— to my grandmother, you have been a pillar for our family. Seeing your strengths has made me want to be stronger.

— to my spiritual father Dr. Kevin A. Williams, your support and mentorship have served at pivotal moments in my life. Your leadership has helped me become more confident, stable and achieve clarity in vision.

— to my uncle Donta Briggs you are an inspiration to me, possessing qualities that I seek to develop within myself. Although you are my uncle, we are more like brothers.

— to my brothers and sisters, I love you all.

To my friends and colleagues, especially:

— to Alice Cheek, Wanda Summers, Desiree Wilkinson, Cory S. Johnson, Nathan D. Cassidy and Ellard Thomas for encouragement, editorial suggestions, feedback and production assistance.

— special thanks to Derrick & Brittany Emanuel, Lauren & Joe Rigsbee, Priscila Jodas Ferreira and Chassidy Robinson for their photo contributions (see book cover).

FOREWARD

Dedrick R. Briggs is a man of integrity, standards, vision and a man of faith. He is one of those tell it like it is friends, and doesn't hold anything back or leave anything to the imagination. The Game of Dating is a no-nonsense book regarding the rules of engagement when it comes to dating itself. Dedrick offers a raw and authentic look at the inner workings of today's single population. He doesn't sugar coat the realities of desperation, brokenness, financial debt, personal baggage, the pressures of social media and their impact on the dating world as it is experienced today.

Take a moment and think about your own personal dating experience and how seriously you have evaluated the potential partners you have allowed to take a place in your life. What do you want out of a mate? What are you willing to put up with? What can they bring to the table or add to your life? According to census.gov, 99.6 million people age 18 and up are unmarried in America today! The issue isn't a lack of singles in the world to date, rather in finding or choosing someone of quality and someone who is best suited for YOU. The Game of Dating helps you address these issues and much more by first taking a look at yourself, your goals, your values and your standards; while defining dating and its stages and styles. Like any infrastructure, organization, group, or important venture, one must first lay a solid foundation. Whether you desire to be married or not, deciding on a mate to be in relationship with for the next year or the subsequent 20 years, requires a process that allows you to weed out the foolishness and distractions in your life. Who you date and who you choose to invite into your life can affect your career, your family and your choices.

The Game of Dating is an etiquette guide and a reality check for the dating society. It provides an honest outlook regarding the barriers and the unnecessary pressures in relationships today. It helps those single and looking, those dating and miserable and those looking to start over better understand what to look for and what to avoid while dating. I, myself, as a single young adult was challenged by the concepts and realities presented in this book. I encourage you to journey through the book with an open mind and willingness to learn. One of my favorite sayings is, "There is ALWAYS room for improvement." Regardless of your past dating experiences, pains or challenges, this book will engage your mind and heart as you gather new information and great nuggets of wisdom to help advance you forward in your dating journey.

Desiree G. Wilkinson, MA
Licensed Professional Counselor Associate

Table of Contents

INTRODUCTION

Renia: "Seriously considering getting a boyfriend. My last relationship ended in October......that's long enough to bounce back right? – March 26, 2011

Beth: "No...."

Brandon: "Ooh yeah, that's too long"

Felicia: "Men only mourn you a week!! So get back in the game!!"

This Facebook post is a question about the appropriate time to get back in what I call, "The Game of Dating". In any game, one must understand the rules and regulations of that game in order to be successful, but that is not all. Most games require strategy and finesse because every decision we make has a consequence. If we are going to be successful, then we must train. Only training specific to the competition will enable us to grow and be victorious.

Have you ever taken the time to consider why people have often been unsuccessful while dating? In this book, we will discuss why many lack success while dating and how we can turn failure into victory. This is not a player's handbook and all that it entails or how to make your girlfriends/boyfriends toes curl, but a book about appropriate dating practices. We will discuss dos, don'ts, and the rules of appropriate dating. Throughout this book, we will hit many different relationship dynamics and situations to acknowledge a variety of issues. Hopefully this edition, in some way, will refer to at least one or more of your issues. If not, don't worry because there is still something in it for you.

Whether one is Divorced, Widowed or fresh in the game, this information will alter your ideas and taste concerning dating. The information in this book will help one become a sophisticated dater, and not someone desperate for attention. As your Coach, my job is not to make decisions for you. My responsibility is to open your eyes to see the most beneficial decisions concerning dating. We must empower and conduct ourselves by more beneficial rules and a profitable standard. Upon completion of this book, you will see relationships in a new light and hold the keys to dating success for your life.

"We all have free choice concerning personal decisions, but before an internal verdict is executed, we must determine whether or not that decision will be what's most beneficial."

Dedrick R. Briggs

Section I
Personal Awareness

Personal awareness is more than being aware of time, place, and events. This individual awareness is an ability intended for reflection. It is the capacity to resolve oneself as an individual separate from their situations and other individuals. Individual awareness helps one assess personal strengths, weaknesses, emotions, beliefs, and motivations. This section is a vital element. Understanding about oneself enables the individual to stand firm on his or her standards and beliefs. In this section, we will explore fundamental topics like developing a mission, vision, and choosing the most beneficial manner to conduct oneself.

CHAPTER 1
SELECT YOUR CHARACTER

In almost every game, one must first choose the most suitable character. In Chess, it is either black or white. There are two types of characters in the Game of Dating, and both have traits that form their individual natures. Each character has a code, one honorable and the other deceptive.

MENSCH vs. IMMORAL

Mensch [MENCH] Dater: An individual concerned with the principles or rules of right conduct. This is not to say that the Mensch does not fall short, but his or her main objective is to do what is right and beneficial for all. The Mensch possesses qualities of honesty, courage, and integrity. When he or she makes mistakes, he or she repents and tries to make things right.

It's easy to be a mensch, his dad said, "You honor your father and mother. You stay married, you set your kids a good example, you don't lie or cheat or steal."

Jane VanDenburgh, Physics of Sunset

Immoral Dater: An individual who engages in illicit or illegal dating activities and often impersonate the Mensch. Like wolves cloaked as sheep, they search for their next victim. An Immoral Dater is selfish and narrow minded. They are not concerned about the long term spiritual, physical and economical wellbeing of others. They are like dogs in heat, blinded by their impulses. The best thing one can do is run.

An Immoral Dater is the modern day Player or Swindler (Gold Digger). A Player to me is like a Juggler. I once saw a Juggler performing with 3 pieces of glass. He was doing well at first, but made a fatal juggler mistake; he only caught one glass. The other two pieces fell to the ground and shattered. That is the result of involving oneself with someone who plays games with your heart. It is just a matter of time before you get dropped.

In the famous Martin Luther King, Jr. speech he said, "I have a dream that my four little children will one day live in a nation where they will not be judged by the color of their skin, but by the content of their character." Regardless of your experiences and views, we are living in the dream of Martin Luther King, Jr. A dream he never got to see or experience. When choosing your character, choose it intelligently.

Chapter 2
Vision Statement

Creating or adopting a personal vision statement is crucial, without personal vision, don't expect success. Relationships ranging from Courting all the way up to Marriage must have a vision statement. While dating one must have an individual vision, unlike those who are married. Their vision statement must include each other. Your vision statement should talk about your future. It must list a realistic image for where you see yourself some years from now, and not things like who you see yourself with in a relationship. It should never say things like, "I see myself with this person, in this size house with 3 children by age 30", especially if you and that person are not dating.

Your vision must give direction about how you will behave, and it should inspire you to give your best. A vision statement communicates both your purpose and core values. Your vision statement has nothing to do with anybody else because it is a reminder of your personal values.

Benefits of a Vision Statement:

- Reminds you of who you are.
- Makes it easier to define actions and goals that will help you achieve your vision.
- Allows you to evaluate yourself. For example, one of your values should be honesty. You will know if you are compromising your vision if you are conducting yourself in dishonesty.

Sometimes vision statements can be difficult to originate, so I have taken the liberty of creating one for you. Feel free to create your own or adopt this one:

COURTSHIP VISION STATEMENT

I will walk in the qualities of integrity (faithfulness, honesty, trustworthiness, commitment, and loyalty). I will be in a good non-abusive relationship with one who embodies the same characteristics as I. I will be a strong communicator, one who listens to their significant other, willing to compromise and come to beneficial resolutions. I will cherish who I am and not surrender my mind or body to be misused. I will walk in forgiveness, forgiving those who have hurt me and I will forgive myself. I will love others, but more importantly I will first love myself.

_____

Signature

Chapter 3
Mission Statement

Unlike the vision statement, concerning where one wants to be, a mission statement emphasizes on how one is going to get there. A mission statement is one of the most basic requirements of a person's life, yet it is frequently overlooked. All people are here to fulfill varying purposes, which should be the core of the mission statement. The only way for a person to continue to improve is by holding themselves responsible, and doing so is unattainable without a clear understanding of individual purpose. Your mission statement should briefly lists the broad goals for how you are going to form acceptable dating habits. Your mission statement must talk about how your day to day practices will get you where you want to be. The mission statement defines your purpose and primary objectives.

Benefits of a Mission Statement:

- Provides personal direction stating what you are about and how you want to be successful.
- Gives focus concentrating on your strengths.
- Can be a guideline for what is acceptable and unacceptable and states your values.
- Challenges you by setting up goals and measurements of achievement for your success.

Sometimes mission statements can be difficult to originate, so I have taken the liberty of creating one for you. Feel free to create your own or adopt this one:

A WOMAN'S COURTSHIP MISSION STATEMENT

I will continually educate myself about appropriate dating habits by reading books, listening to audios and/or not being ashamed to ask for advice. My purpose for dating is to be found by a suitable man. To accomplish this, I will be faithful to myself first and not make excuses. I will live my life as an expression of the principals I believe and be guided by my values and beliefs. I will be vocally expressive of my values and not deviate because of the expectations of others. I will conduct myself as a lady not allowing others to tear me down because I have chosen to act within my individual purpose. I will immediately disconnect from any man that will verbally abuse me. I will show Men what respect for me looks like, encouraging that person of interest to end dates around a certain time and focus solely on getting to know one another. I will take my time, and I will not let others rush me to date, have sex or get married.

A MAN'S COURTSHIP MISSION STATEMENT

I will continually educate myself about appropriate dating habits by reading books, listening to audios and/or not being ashamed to ask for advice. My purpose for dating is to find a suitable woman. To accomplish this, I will be faithful to myself first and not make excuses. I will live my life as an expression of the principals I believe and be guided by my values and beliefs. I will be vocally expressive of my values and not deviate because of the expectations of others. Because I have chosen to act within my individual purpose, I will walk in manliness not allowing others to emasculate me. I will show women what true respect and maturity looks like. I will end my dates at a respectable time and focus solely on getting to know that person of interest. I will take my time, and I will not let others rush me to date, have sex or get married.

CHAPTER 4
UNIQUE, COMPLETE & WHOLE
"BEING SUCCESSFULLY SINGLE"

"If I am looking for the rest of me within someone else, I am setting myself and my relationship up for failure."

Victoria Fleming, Ph.D.

N ever use expressions describing your significant other as your other-half or your better-half. Statements like that produce a psychosomatic notion that you are incomplete without a significant other. Singleness has never denoted incompleteness, but a state of oneness. Incompleteness, by definition, is a condition of deficiency; lack; or neediness. This psychological model locks us in a co-dependent state of mind, encouraging us to rely on others for emotional wellbeing and stability. Being single is a gift that affords one time to learn about oneself, build individuality and self worth. It is the state when one can learn how to be independent, build character and admirable qualities. Piecing self worth qualities like honesty, trustworthiness, loyalty, commitment, and faithfulness together transforms one from the average to the exceptional. When you say 'I am Single', essentially you are definitively saying, "I have all the required parts or elements. I emotionally lack nothing and I have all the required or expected characteristics that make me entire." An important element to have is awareness through identity, and I believe learning oneself is the requirement to success within this process. If you don't know who you are, why would you expect anyone else to know? If one does not have vision and purpose, he or she may never amount to anything.

Expression through one's unique identity and not mimicking someone else is what makes one distinctive from others. Intimate knowledge of oneself enables them not to be easily swayed because he or she understands their purpose. I have witnessed many relationship casualties because one or both went in seeking identity, purpose and vision from the other person. When we go into relationships with deep implanted insecurities and double-mindedness it only destroys the potential within the relationship.

As we develop our own individuality, we'll grow confident in our capability to handle whatever challenges come our way; it is what separates the Hero's from the Sidekicks. Instead of naively running into mischief or fleeing for fear, we'll face challenges confidently, intelligently and with wisdom.

THE STAGE OF PREPARATION

Louis Greenup said it best, "Singleness is pre-season training and if you are not successful in the pre-season you won't be successful in the Game." Remember, this isn't just about dating, but rather becoming a sophisticated dater. As an unmarried individual, it is vital that one focus on increasing knowledge, self-worth, and strive for financial stability and comfort.

A better You will attract the best for you, but it all begins with the fundamentals of being unique, complete and whole. So what contributes to so many relationship casualties? I believe it is because people get back into the game ill-equipped. When you lack totality, you will allow people to handle you inappropriately and that's why improving oneself and understanding this game is vital. Dating is not a race; and, finishing the quickest should never be the goal.

REALITY CHECK Q&A

How does one avoid making some of the mistakes made by many people?

I have a simple reply: Build your self-worth. Building emotional security enables you to be independent and less codependent. When dating we give just enough to see if it has the potential to go to the next level. While hoping for an engagement ring, I've seen women continue to have babies. I've also seen men blow savings and waste prosperity because they fell in love with a woman that didn't value the significance of saving and sophisticated investing. I have not begun to mention those who are courting or in an exclusive relationship, but their hearts are still with previous Exes. When one lacks completeness it's like having an unfinished puzzle set. Lacking wholeness is like having that same puzzle set, but the person who gave it to you still has some of the pieces. Key indicators that you are not entire are feelings of emptiness, insecurity or inadequacy. Those emotions are like gaping holes or voids and when felt, one usually by means of desperation tries to fill them. Unfortunately it's often through temporary means of satisfaction.

Essentially, in order to be complete one must first reach the state of wholeness and to be whole you must have all of the puzzle pieces. Stephen R. Covey probably illustrates how to accomplish this best in his book, "7 Habits of Highly Effective People."

I DON'T NEED YOU, BUT I WANT YOU

As insensitive as this may sound, that is what I told my wife while we were dating. By this time a little maturity had sunk in, and I recognized that I truly did not need a significant other to feel happy about myself. I encouraged her to pursue success and wealth for herself, whether it was through going back to school, a career or building a successful business. I encouraged her to seek independence because I wanted her to be successful whether I was present or not. I did not wish for her to need me, my desire was for her to want me.

I believe when couples realize they don't need each other for emotional fulfillment or to reach a state of financial security, it increases their success rate. I believe that being whole is not just a matter of being in excellent emotional health, but it also includes having success within what I call your Personal Economy (P.E.). An economy consists of a social network where goods and services are exchanged according to supply and demand, along with the management of the resources of that community or country. Just like a country has an economy, so does your personal life. So what does recession indicate within an economy? Recession is an indication that there are weak points within that financial system. Bad Credit History and a high debt to income ratio are all indicators that your P.E. is in a recession.

When people come to me for dating advice I often ask them two questions. The first is usually, is your Personal Economy in order? That subject frequently leads into my next concern: "Why are you giving so

much attention to Dating when you are living pay check to pay check?"
Give more attention to building your personal economy, instead. This
means before you give yourself entirely into dating, consider taking more
time to get your P.E. in order.

"Cherish your singleness because it affords you the time to make yourself
disciplined and successful."

Dedrick R. Briggs

The goal of every single person should be to reach a state of financial
security and comfort. Why be single, financially broke with high debt and
poor credit? As stated before, singleness affords you the time to achieve
success. If everyone sought to enhance their own P.E., there would be no
gold diggers. Why seek companionship for money? Get your own money.
It is essential to keep your ducks in a row. Gentlemen, accomplish what
your fathers before you did not. Get out of "survival mode" and go after
success and stability. Ladies, stop waiting on that Knight in shining armor
to take care of you for the rest of your lives. Go after success and stability
for yourselves; you should always be able to contribute something of value
to the relationship.

REALITY CHECK QUIZ

Over and over again I see people get caught up in their significant
other to the point they neglect their responsibilities and commitments.
When did giving up on your dreams and goals become the prerequisite
for building a successful relationship? I've seen people get fired because
the times they should have been working, they were spending it with
their significant other. I've witnessed many college students flunk out of
school because the times they should have been in class or studying, they

were sleeping in longer with their Beau.

I often encourage others to give most of their attention to their goals and aspirations prior to seeking companionship. If the relationship is for you, then he or she will be there when you are done achieving success. Besides, do you really want a person who is not willing to sacrifice so you have the time and focus to achieve your ambitions?

SO THE REALITY CHECK QUESTION IS:

Is dating more important to me than being unique, complete & whole?

Yes _____ No_____

You may say I can do both, and you are right, you can. By no means am I telling you not to date; but, as stated previously, I am encouraging you to make the most beneficial decisions and not decisions based on popularity. Socially popular dating methods encourage us to impress those we are dating, even if we go broke in the process.

Think about it.

What does it say about you when you cannot properly meet financial deadlines after wining & dining a date? Sadly, many are more concerned about wining & dining, than they are about taking care of their most important responsibilities. Unfortunately, many social popular dating methods encourage us to seek self worth, and identity from companionship. To be frank, you are worthless to anyone if you lack individuality. While we're trying to figure out who we are that person has two options: wait or move on to the next prospect. When one lacks identity, one lacks substance. When one lacks substance, one lacks value. Very similar to the college senior that has changed their major several times, and still doesn't know what they want to do.

Obviously, this requirement goes both ways. Not only should we seek to be entire, we should be able to identify whether or not someone of interest has uniqueness and is complete and whole. I cannot count the number of people who had a lot going for them, but got with someone that did not, and it brought them down. Oftentimes, when we bring others into our circle of influence, it can cause digression if their game is not up to par. As individuals seeking long term companionship, it is our responsibility to bring our A-game, not the bare minimum.

FACEBOOK QUOTE

"If you can't handle being single, then you can't handle being in a relationship."

Maranda Coltrane

Chapter 5
Starting Over

In some way, we have all had to start over. We have all suffered from a broken heart, rejection and much more. Dr. Drew said, "Relationships early in life are kind of designed to come and go." It is imperative that we grasp and embrace the reality that no matter how much we want certain relationships to work, some will not work. For whatever reasons, you will often find yourself starting over repetitively, but you are not alone. There is always someone who has or is going through the same situation or something similar.

Starting over is not the same for each person. Some may go through a serious break up, divorce, or death of a spouse; and, many experience this with children. Those getting back into the dating game, with children, face a much more difficult challenge. I once heard someone say, "Starting over feels like life hit the restart button, midway during a 20 mile marathon." This is heart wrenching for many because in their mind, they have found "The One". They never imagined they would be back in a competition they fought so hard to escape. When we think we've found The One, we hold on tight, even if the relationship is not beneficial. Our deficiency in determining the long term benefit for others in our lives has proven to be our Achilles heel. Usually, we look for temporary satisfactions. Initially, we consider looks and what they can do for us or to us. In the early stages of dating, it is always better to assume that the person of interest is not The One until the relationship has been tested and has some tenure.

Many singles, with no children, are likely to encounter those who have children from previous relationships or marriages due to the high divorce rate and the growing number of children born outside of wedlock. For that reason, it is vital to appreciate that one's children must always come first. If you can see yourself with a person who already has children, then engage all areas of their life, including their offspring. If you're not into the instant-family thing, then steer clear of that relationship dynamic. You cannot just come into the life of that person and not expect to have an active role in the life of his or her children. All those I have interviewed made it abundantly clear: If someone cannot accept his or her child, then he or she is not an option for him or her.

I launched an opinion poll and received many relevant and enlightening responses. I took the liberty of including several responses to encourage you. I received a powerful statement from Alexis Alexander, a single mother and successful student currently attending Winston Salem State University. She said, "…set standards, be firm, know what you want, and have patience. When you have a child and you are seeking to date again, you have to have standards for yourself and around your child. Your number one question should be "Can this person be a good role model for my child?" If you are dating and have been for some time, it has to get to a point where that person makes an effort to get to know your child; because, he or she can't date you and expect for that to be all. He or she has to date the child too! If you have someone that doesn't date the child; then, they're not The One. Also, the significant other and child should have an effortless relationship where neither is being forced; but, the most important is taking your time and getting to know the person. Stick to your standards in what you want and don't settle out of desperation. Dating is complicated enough, but dating with children is even more complicated."

Alexis hit some points that many should consider and process within their mental database. Needless to say, these issues and circumstances are throughout all ages: Teenagers are getting pregnant habitually, married couples with 20 years plus are divorcing, and many others are battling with the decision. As stated before, proper keys and principles are essential for anyone of any stage to successfully move through the dating game. In other words, success in this game requires honest commitment and adherence to the proper code of ethics.

WORDS OF ENCOURAGEMENT

If you've lost someone through a break-up, divorce or death, "I would tell them that it is a process that takes time to cope and reestablish who you are. It is difficult to start over; but, it is even harder when there are kids involved. I suggest keeping things in perspective: If it is hard for you; then, imagine how hard it is for the child. It is also important to remember that it's ok to grieve. It is ok to have weak moments; however, you have to rest assure that God has your back. With time, heartache will heal and He will bless you with happiness; but, it may not be with a relationship."

Amber Johnson

"Well, first let me say any man that dates me would have to understand and be ok with the fact that I have a child and my child is part of me .... I know it could be hard for a person to accept a child that is not his/her own; but, if he or she loves that person; then, they will come to love that child. They would definitely need to get to know the child. For a person who is "starting over," the same applies; but, it's all about getting to know that person and spending time with them."

Tia Steens

To be considerate of someone who is not my child's biological parent, "…I believe that it's important not to bring that person around your child until you know that there is potential for a long term relationship. I guess ultimately I would be considerate by ensuring that he doesn't enter my child's life unless we are both ready for what that means."

Amber Johnson

"Straight up real talk: For a man anything we fail at is hard. It's what I call the "Hero Syndrome", where every man dreams of being someone's hero. That is why we grow up idolizing super heroes, the police, fireman, etc. When something like a relationship fails it's a hard blow. Divorce especially, but when moving on, the inward battle has to be won first. In every war, high ground is always best. High ground is the truth and facing the truth. Of course, it's not always your fault. But you always consider what you could have done better in order to make self-improvements. Never look to move on immediately. Take time to heal and fix yourself; because, if you don't, you will not be beneficial for the next relationship. There is life after divorce. Instead of thinking about what the other person did wrong, focus on becoming a better person."

Michael Brice

Section II
Dating 101

Before one can excel in anything, one has to learn the basics. As it pertains to the realm of sophisticated dating, many of us expect to walk before we crawl. The fundamentals of successful dating are in the rules that govern it. If we do not abide by those rules, then we forfeit the protection and success they reward us. Have you ever tried to put something together without reading the instructions? Of course you have. Essentially, that is what you are doing when you do not educate yourself about appropriate dating practices. What would happen if someone did not follow the rules of their job? They would likely be disciplined or terminated. If we choose not to abide by the rules within dating, then we will constantly face the risk of failure.

Essentially, many of us have miserably failed at proper Dating. In school when a student fails a test, he does not immediately retake the test. A wise student always takes time to study and prepare. A wise student always decides to sophisticate or refine their understanding about subject matters in order to be successful. Before you try again, educate yourself. More importantly discipline your heart, and then get back in the game.

CHATER 6

THE DEFINITION OF DATING

Definition is everything; and, it is the catalyst to understanding. Understanding provides clarity, enabling us to make the most advantageous choices. Oftentimes, our choices are influenced by our exposure to information. Getting the wrong information could be the reason why some of the decisions we have made, while dating, have not been the best. Joan Didion said, "Read, learn, work it up, and go to the literature. Information is control." Here is your first assignment. Before we discuss definition, take a moment and think about this question.

WHAT IS DATING?

SEE INSTRUCTIONS BELOW:

- Step 1: Take about 10 second to think about my question, then proceed to step 2. Ready, set, go.
- Step 2: Now compare your definition to my own below.

The true meaning of dating comes from the word data (pronounced DAY-ta, or DA-ta). Data is the Latin plural of datum, meaning "to give." The definition of romantic dating, in its purest form, means to collect information about and from a potential companion. Dating also requires a yielding of information on the part of each prospect. Dating may be a private matter between two people or may be a public affair. Traditionally, it is the role of a man to court, pursue or "woo" a woman. As a result, this may encourage her interest in him, and receptiveness to further interpersonal development.

Dating never ends, because who your significant other was 10 years ago, is not who they are today. As we age, mature through understanding and experiences; it requires us to learn one another on different levels. Essentially, the foundation of all relationship stages is dating.

CHAPTER 7
STUDENT OF DATING

Unfortunately within the western culture, dating has become somewhat of a lost art. Dating is a time of searching, investigation, discovery, and adventure, not escapade. For that reason, when dating, one must adopt the mindset of a student.

STUDENT

A person formally engaged in learning; any person who studies, investigates or examines thoughtfully.

When students are in school, they should not attend classes for a refund check. Students must acquire information and understanding. When we have information and understanding, it increases our value. We become marketable based on our knowledge. What is the worth of a surgeon that doesn't understand Anatomy? His worth is based on his knowledge. It is no different within a dating relationship. Your worth increases based on your knowledge and understanding about the person you are dating. While dating, one must gather information, and seek to understand. Unfortunately, the modern rules governing relationships and romance are informal and vague. When a couple schedules a date night, they will do various things like go to a movie, have dinner, or go dancing. Regrettably, many no longer simply sit and talk, or seek to learn the other person. I often encourage couples to go to places where they can sit and discuss each other's interest, and authentically get to know the other person. Don't date as if you have it all figured out.

Courtship is comparative to academic studying; and, an appropriate study environment is essential to further one's educational success. Why do you think most people study in private-based settings, like their room or the library? Those environments are quiet, serene and predictable. The more information one retains, the more capable they will be of obtaining their goals. No one, of reasonable thought, would host a study group at a rock concert; but, that's where we go on dates. Do not misunderstand me; group dating has its place; however, if you are seriously interested in someone, spend quality time with them alone.

The logic behind group dating is to learn how a person of interest will interact with family, friends and associates. Inadvertently, a poll is taken to see if this new person has a chance. The best way to learn about someone is within a private-based setting. It is okay to get the opinions of family and others; but, they cannot make the decision for you. Sometimes we need the opinion of Mom or Dad to say, "I don't think they're the one for you." Essentially, that is what we are doing when we allow others to dictate the majority of our relationship decisions. Only a person who lacks understanding says, "I have a major exam tomorrow, can you study for me?" Having the courage to study a prospect for oneself, is a very powerful inner strength. Get out of the mindset of letting other's do the work for you. We have to stop making excuses for not knowing the people we interact with on a daily basis. While dating, always seek to gather information; it is how you learn the value of others for your life.

"…Information is control."

Joan Didion

Chapter 8

Stages of Development

One evening while working I received a call from an associate. The first thing he said to me was, "Hey, I think I messed up." I responded, "Ok…What did you do?" He said, "Do you remember that girl Jasmine I told you about? Well, she's all mad and doesn't want to be with me anymore." He went on to tell me that they were at his house with another couple when an unexpected visitor came to his home. He told Jasmine he was going outside to handle an issue; but, when he returned Jasmine had left. When he called her, she told him, it was over because she did not appreciate how he left her inside with the other couple. She went on to tell him that she was sacrificing a lot just to spend time with him; and, there was nothing he could do to make it up to her. "How long have you two been dating," I asked him. He replied, "Two weeks."

While dating, each person must acknowledge that dating is the initial stage of learning a person. The initial stage should never be regarded as critically as a tenured monogamous relationship. When I hear about couples having issues while dating, it is a red flag to me. When people get frustrated while dating, and there are no exclusive commitments or titles, I usually deliver sobering responses like: "Why are you angry? You are only dating. It's not like you're married." I encourage them to view their connection for what it is.

Initially, you would think that Jasmine is demanding respect. In my opinion, when a person responds in that manner, it is seldom an issue of respect. It is typically a matter of maintaining a level of control. More often than not, in the beginning stage of dating, we are testing the water: What can I get away with or how far can I go with this person? Respect is a major factor in any relationship and must be reciprocated between both people. You will always be able to tell when a person wants respect. They will address you with mutual respect in order to come to a profitable resolution. If a beneficial decision cannot be agreed on, then separation is the next step. According to the information provided, Jasmine had a temper tantrum and stormed out instead of communicating her concerns. Like undisciplined children, when things are not going their way, they will often cry, yell and act unruly. When they get what they want, they realign their character. When a child consistently acquires their desires by temper tantrums, this immature conduct continues into adulthood until they meet people who will not tolerate their behavior.

I am a firm believer that appropriately distinguishing between interpersonal courtship stages while dating, enables one to keep a grip on reality. Progression to one person may not be the same for the other person. Mutual understanding and communication are imperative in order to sustain a reciprocated outlook about your relationship status. Described below are various descriptions for the stages of development within relationships. They will help you gain a better understanding and identify your specific relationship stage.

STAGE I: INCIPIENT STAGE

This stage is also known as the Introduction Stage. When a man approaches a woman, one of two things will happen "something or nothing". If nothing happens this is an indication that one or both people are mutually uninterested, at this point the potential for further development ceases. If something happens there will be what most identify as that spark, signifying there is a mutual interest and intention toward progression.

a.   PHASE 1: INEBRIATION

After the Introduction Stage, feelings usually progress toward the first phase, also known as the Butterfly Phase. This is the phase when you are head-over-heels for the other person, and they absolutely can do no wrong. This is best described as the stage of intoxication or bliss. Like an inebriated person, one will begin to exhibit slight irregular behavior or reduced inhibition. Reduced inhibition is a term in psychology used to describe a lack of restraint that can manifest in different ways, including:

> i. Disregard for social conventions: This is when one becomes inclined to do things that most would consider inappropriate.
>
> ii. Impulsivity/Poor Risk Assessment: One is less likely to consider or regard the consequences for bad decisions
>
> iii. Hypersexuality: There is an increase in sexual urges or sexual activity. One is more inclined to be sexually involved with someone.
>
> iv. Hyperphagia: You eat more. People often gain weight when they are comfortable in a relationship.

b.   PHASE 2: SOBERING

After the first phase we begin to come off of the emotional high. When one reaches this stage, one starts to see the other person for who he or she really is and not through the gaze of ecstasy.

STAGE II: GROWTH STAGE

This stage is what I consider the 'Make It or Break It' Stage. That same spark you felt when you first met has become flames. This is a crucial stage in which one truly begins to get to learn the good, bad, ugly, and what one will or will not tolerate from that person. During this stage people often move forward into engagement. The couple may not have publically declared intentions to marry; but, they sure are acting like it. Oftentimes, there's a form of substandard betrothal, usually indicated by a promise ring or other symbol. It is from this point that a relationship can go one of two ways: to the Fully Developed Stage or to the Decay stage.

STAGE III: FULLY DEVELOPED STAGE

This stage is the point of selflessness and mature love. Typically, this is seen within a tenured marriage. The couple has spent most of their time learning and seeking to understand one another. In this stage, you are still learning about the other person, but you have a concrete understanding of their goals, temperament and how they would respond to most things.

STAGE EX: DECAY STAGE

This is the stage when progress toward or within a relationship flat lines. Arguments, emotional grief, and ultimately breakups occur and the relationship dissolves. Unresolved issues and/ or inappropriate behavior are usually the cause for the decline in the relationship. This stage requires more boundaries than all the others combined, because they become your Ex.

Dedrick R. Briggs

STAGES OF DEVELOPMENT
PROGRESSION CHART

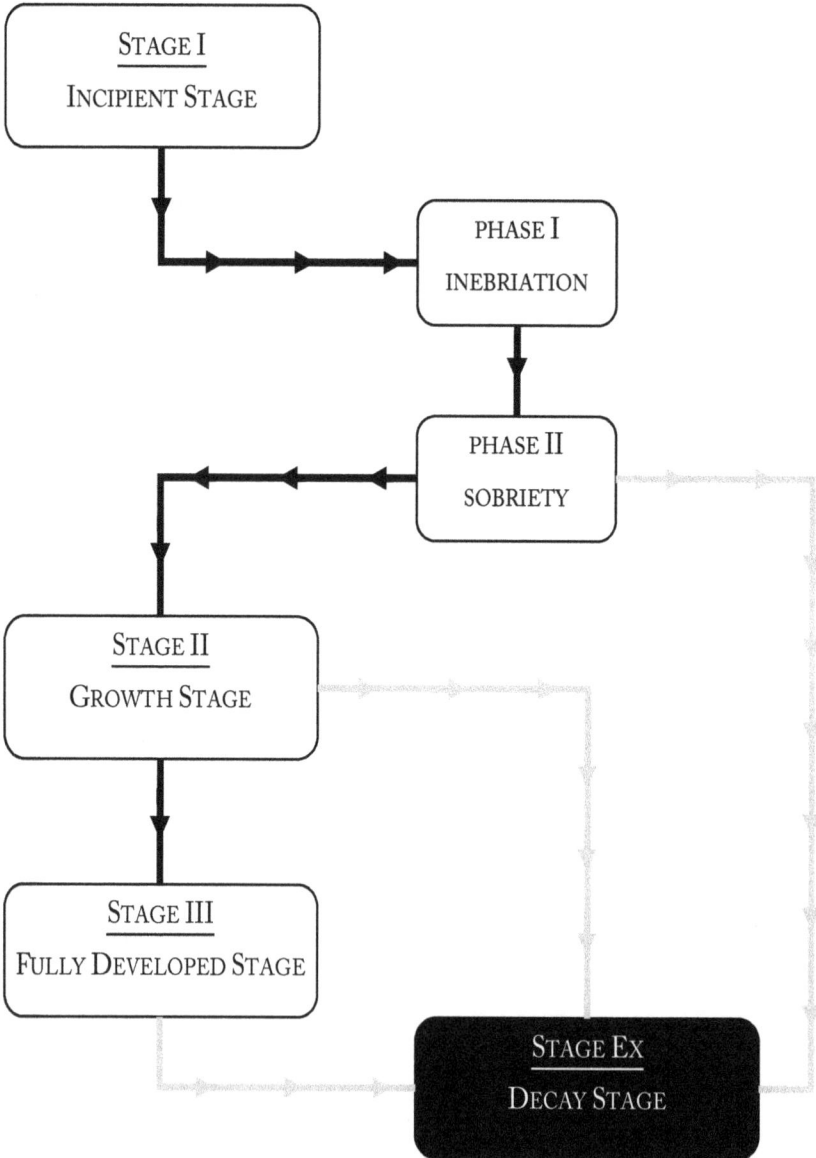

```
┌─────────────────────┐
│      STAGE I         │
│   INCIPIENT STAGE    │
└─────────────────────┘
           │
           ▼────────────────►    ┌─────────────────┐
                                 │     PHASE I      │
                                 │   INEBRIATION    │
                                 └─────────────────┘
                                          │
                                          ▼
           ◄────────────────    ┌─────────────────┐
           │                    │    PHASE II      │
           ▼                    │    SOBRIETY      │
┌─────────────────────┐         └─────────────────┘
│     STAGE II         │
│   GROWTH STAGE       │
└─────────────────────┘
           │
           ▼
┌─────────────────────┐         ┌─────────────────┐
│    STAGE III         │         │    STAGE EX      │
│ FULLY DEVELOPED STAGE│         │   DECAY STAGE    │
└─────────────────────┘         └─────────────────┘
```

CHAPTER 9
GENDER ROLES

Look at how it stands, so confident and bold. I've seen it in action, it's powerful and strong. Its style and finesse unseen in the land. What sort is this kind?

HE called him Man.

The design of a man is to provide, protect and love. Oftentimes, these characteristics are confidently and effortlessly executed. According to a more traditional standard, men are supposed to pursue the woman. To pursue a thing means to: (1) engage, (2) follow up or proceed with (3) to find or employ measures to obtain.

1. Men, when you engage a woman, you have to captivate her. In exchange for her interest, you also give her yours. A woman of integrity wants to know if you are genuinely interested. She is no different than any other woman. When she dreams, her dreams are big and specific. I can hear my wife say, "Every woman wants that big wedding; I've dreamed of it since I was like five." If this applies to most women; then, most women probably have a clear idea of what they want in companionship.

2.   When you make the decision to, as the older generations call it "court a woman", the initial phase requires getting to know her. Use various forms of communication that are convenient for her, like phone calls, texting, video chatting or emailing. Relationships are built by proper communication and maintained by trust. Generally, before we assume relationship titles, we identify prospects as friends. After dating for a while, she will want to know where the friendship is going: Are you looking to have an open relationship or do you want to have an exclusive relationship? These questions and more are important to discuss in order to prevent confusion and hurt feelings.

"Talking to girls is easy, they'll tell you everything. The secret to talking to girls, is listening."

We Bought A Zoo

3. After you have captured her attention, take her out on dates. This is another phase of courting. Take her to a nice dine-in restaurant, host a picnic, or go walking in a garden or on the beach. If you like her, use appropriate measures to "woo" and retain her. In order to be on the same page, exchange expectations. Consider what you are going to do to build and maintain trust. This is something women look for in a prospective husband. A woman of lasting substance will want to be approached by a respectable man who is confident. Women understand that men have to maintain the leadership role. If you are what she considers a suitable package, she will, hopefully, align herself and contribute everything she has to offer.

Much gentler than that of the Man, yet their power is alike and to will it can. Much different in anatomy, the matrix is within. What sort is this kind?

he called her Woman,
"MOTHER OF ALL MAN"

The traditional approach is the advance of any respectable man. Women must learn to get hip to the game without violating the rules within dating. Cut out the aggressive pursuits geared toward capturing a man. In the days of old, men had to hunt for everything; so, by nature men are hunters. They would go out, stalk their prey, capture it and bring it home to feast.

Hunting was not an easy task. What doe, in its right mind, lies down as if to say, "Take me home; I'm all yours." Have you ever seen a fish not put up a fight? A good catch never makes it easy for the man. As odd as it sounds, Ladies, you are The Catch. While you are waiting, it is important not to make yourself easy prey for every hunter that comes your way. Every man that preys on you, prior to the arrival of your valiant hunter, has the potential to decrease your value. A good man is looking for a suitable woman that understands her worth, one who will not allow others to treat her as if she is disposable or useless.

When a man is ready to settle down, he'll start "Catching and Releasing". This is a term used in fishing when fishermen catch fish, and then let them go. Generally, if he throws her back, it is because he identified her as an unsuitable catch. The hunter is looking for a prize fish, one with a little fight in her. He wants one that can look good beside him in a photo; and, when he has the need to feed, he can delight in her for days. Women fail to realize every man likes a good hunt; and, he is searching for that one and only special catch. He may have caught some things here and there, but they do not compare to you.

Hundreds of years ago, women knew how to seize the attention of a man without appearing easy. If a man noticed a woman dropped something, like her handkerchief, he would go out of his way to pick it up and hand it to her. If she had her eye on a particular man, she might intentionally drop her handkerchief, in an effortless attempt to get his attention. This was no doubt a clever method, somewhat of an elegant pursuit. Think about it, she baits him; and, if he likes what he sees, he goes after her. This kind of woman doesn't go running up to a man like a groupie, throwing herself at him because of his status or appearance. Instead, she lets the man come after her.

This is an important quality for women to have. Women who chase men only contribute to their obliteration. If he doesn't work to captivate you, he is less likely to appreciate you. This is not a man thing, it is simply human nature. One is less likely to appreciate what one has never had to work to attain.

As a lady you must be attractive without looking desperate or easy. You must not lie down like the dumb doe. You must become skilled at letting the man chase you; but, do not run too fast. Give yourself the opportunity to be caught by a suitable man.

CHAPTER 10
CANDIDATES

When there is a mutual interest to date, both people become prospects or what I call candidates. A candidate is a person who seeks an office, like the President of the United States. Consider the election of Presidential candidates. They are nothing more than ordinary people, who have met the customary requirements of consideration to be elected as head of government for the United States. After they have met the necessary requirements to run for president, they then have to campaign or win the support of those electing them. Dating is no different. One may have a host of candidates, some more than others, who campaign for their vote; but, a wise voter listens to the views and beliefs of all the candidates.

After learning the importance of voting, I began following the Presidential candidate debates throughout the years. I observed the candidates' confidence and assertiveness, and how they reacted under pressure. I considered their background, current achievements, reputation, how they handled other candidates, and how they even handled the current president. More importantly, I listened attentively to their expressed beliefs, values, vision and goals. After the completion of my assessment, there comes the fundamental question: Who do I think will be the best candidate for me? I have to make a decision that is not based on the views of my family, friends or associates.

Before one considers an exclusive relationship, one must send each candidate through that same process of elimination. One must assess several personality traits like:

- CHARACTER: What are their moral and ethical qualities and do they behave within those ethics? It is important to access and compare how they behave in public and private settings. Is their character consistent? Are they moody or happy? Do they exhibit low self-esteem or a healthy perspective about life and self?

• BELIEFS: Core beliefs affect expectations in relationships; so, it's imperative to know whether or not their ethical convictions align with your own. If their beliefs or views make you cringe; they may not be the person for you.

• VISION: Where do they see themselves in one to five years or ten years? I cannot stress the importance of choosing someone with a clear plan for his or her life. No one has all the answers and our futures are never truly certain; but, they should have a plan. When people answer with I-Don't-Know or they have no clue where they want to be, they are not ready for anything serious; and; they will only be a distraction to you.

• GOALS: What do they plan to accomplish short and long term? Unfortunately, people without a vision must first get a vision and a plan before they will be able to execute goals and benchmarks.

• BACKGROUND: What are their accomplishments? Where did they go to school? Where do they work? Ask questions because that is the only way you are going to learn about the candidate.

• REPUTATION: How are they viewed within their community, family and among friends? It is not very difficult to assess the reputation of others. Just take your time, keep your eyes & ears open; and, do not be afraid to casually discuss things about them with their family and friends.

• SOCIAL INTERACTION: How do they treat others? Someone who treats their family, friends and associates appropriately will likely treat you with mutual respect.

I have an associate who enjoys fine dining. Occasionally, he will take a date to the finest restaurant in the city. How she handles their server determines whether or not they continue their date. In the Game of Dating, you will come across many different candidates; and, if their character, lifestyle, vision, goals and beliefs align with your own; then, it is okay to mark your ballot. Don't date others for good looks or because others think they are a terrific catch. Date them because it is evident they can add value to your life.

CHAPTER 11

CATEGORICAL RELATIONSHIPS

"The importance of distinguishing between relationships is as important as knowing the location of an emergency flash light during a power outage."

#DRBRIGGS

Distinguishing between social connections is very important, because it helps one to remain logical about the various relationships in his or her life. For that reason, I do not call everyone friend; and, those I come in contact with, are usually sorted within the associate category.

A friend is someone you know well, trust, and who has proven to be consistently reliable. When you say this is my friend, you are saying, "I know this person and have full knowledge of them clearly and with certainty." This issue was blurred within the social network of Facebook for years. Everyone you linked with was classified as a friend, even if you never met them. It took the developers of Facebook several years to establish a profile setting that differentiated friends from acquaintances. Near the end of 2011, Facebook launched new updates to the social network, giving users the capability to create and sort various links within suitable relationship categories, such as:

- Close friends
- Acquaintances
- Same High School or College
- Same City
- Work colleagues, etc.

With more control over their Facebook profiles, users were able to categorize their thousands of social links. Facebook made things easy by acknowledging a reality they neglected for years. Unfortunately, this reality remains blurred within the interpersonal relationships of many people.

Recently, a young lady messaged me on Facebook, wanting advice about her new relationship. Her message stated, "I'm having some problems with my boyfriend. We've been arguing a lot. I really like him and don't want to lose him. PLEASE HELP!" She continued on by telling me that they have been together for a few months, but were clashing a lot lately. When I responded, I asked her how long they had known each other. She said, "I've known him all my life, ever since elementary school." I asked her if they had remained connected since elementary school. She replied, "No. After elementary school, I moved; but, I recently met him again at a party three months ago…"

STOP!

Let's back track. Do you remember her telling me that they have known each other all of their lives? She neglected to tell me that the last time she saw him was about 10 years ago, and now she is in college. This is my point: They do not know one another at this place in their relationship. Their current familiarity was founded on their childhood. Can you honestly say that who you are today is the same person you were 10 years ago? Henri Bergson said, "To exist is to change, to change is to mature, to mature is to go on creating oneself endlessly." Both people went through a 10 year transformation. It is delusional to meet someone over a decade later or even a year, and believe that you still know that person.

As important as it is to categorize relationships, it is more beneficial to give our relationships time to develop and mature. Have you ever seen that person tremendously angry and under an excessive amount of stress? If you answered no, then you do not know them as well as you think you do. I know many people who have ended up with children or gotten married under these same self-made fairy tales. Now, instead of the relationship just working, they always have to make it work. They said, they were "in love"; but, when that emotion faded, and the butterflies had flown away, they realized they had no clue who they were laying beside. Don't be the individual who continually puts people in places they do not belong. Protect yourself by placing others in their appropriate relationship category.

SUITABILITY

Me: "Hey, James. Long time, no see. How's everything going?"

James: "It's going alright, I guess. It's not really working out with that girl I told you about. We're just not compatible."

Me: "James, I didn't FB you to talk about your relationship."

James: "Well, you asked how I as doing."

Me: "Well, you've only been dating her for a few months; give it some time. You know your patience is as thin as a sheet of paper. You sure it's not just because it's getting close to Christmas time, and you're trying to avoid having to buy gifts?" LOL!!!

James: "Come on man. Be serious."

Me: "Ok, my bad. Serious face ☺ LOL!!!!!!!!!"

James: "Ha, ha, ha, funny. You don't get it bruh. We're complete opposites. For example: I like going to church on Sundays but, she'd rather stay home and watch HGTV."

Me: "Hey. Don't hate on HGTV, I love those shows. Besides, what's wrong with that?"

James: "Everything! You know my beliefs; and, going to church to learn is very important to me. Every once in a while, I could understand; but, she NEVER wants to go. Don't let me get on her car and apartment...dirty, filthy, and nasty. I didn't know women like that existed. I think I should break it off before I waste anymore time. We just don't fit..."

James is obviously expressing his dismay concerning the lack of suitability between himself and the person he is dating. James used the word compatible, which means the capability to exist or live together in harmony. Living in harmony is achievable among all mankind, but a more appropriate term is suitability. The reason many relationships do not work is due to the lack of suitability.

According to Leslie Baxter & Barbara Montgomery's Dimensions of the Dialectic, relationships revolve around the ways in which we communicate with each other. The relationship dialectics theory argues that people in a relationship experience dynamic tensions between pairs of opposing motives or desires. In laymen's terms, these are areas of conflict or disagreement. I believe this also extends to one's beliefs. Before entering any level of relationship, it is important to assess suitability by examining areas of conflict. If you eventually want to get married and have children, but they do not want to; then, that is an area of conflict. If you are neat and tidy, but they are not; then, that is an area of conflict. Areas of conflict contribute to stress and eventually dissension within relationships. If you are unable to reach agreeable compromises while dating; then, it is most beneficial to disconnect before the relationship progresses.

Major causative factors in the decay of many relationships are lack of suitability and lack of positive contributions. While evaluating candidates, one must also ask oneself if this person can positively contribute to my life? It is very simple. People entering your life, over time, will either contribute positively or negatively. Gayle King was able to have her own television show on the Oprah Winfrey Network because of her relationship with the talk show icon. Gayle then moved on to host on CBS This Morning. If you look at Oprah's Twitter account on January 9, 2012 12:48pm, you'll see a statement of support:

Oprah Oprah Winfrey

Morning tweeps...I'm up early to watch CBS morning show. Gayle's debut. For 25 years she watched my show while working out, now I will.

Who was Gayle before Oprah? A positive, contributing relationship enabled Gayle to reach heights she possibly would have never seen without the appropriate connection. It's not about fame or fortune, but about becoming the best person you can be. The question you must ask yourself is, "Can this candidate help me progress closer to where I need to be?" It's not enough just to be present, provide physical stimulation or subsidize necessities. When the rubber hits the road, you need to know whether or not a candidate has what it takes to help you be the best.

CHAPTER 13
EXCLUSIVE VS. OPEN

It is imperative that a mutual manner of courtship be determined and communicated. If two people cannot agree on what I call a dating style, and it be honored by both people, it is best to disconnect. If one prefers to be in an exclusive relationship, and the other prefers the opposite, conduct while dating will likely cause hurt feelings and drama. In this chapter, we will briefly discuss styles of dating and how to distinguish between each method.

MONO-DATING

Mono-dating is also known as exclusive dating and refers to the state of courting only one person at a time. It is drawn from the word monogamy, which is a term applied to marriage in which an individual has only one spouse at any one time.

THIS STYLE OF DATING IS ACCEPTABLE

POLY-DATING

Poly-dating, which is also known as open dating, originates from the term polygamy, which refers to the state of dating more than one person at a time. There are two styles of Poly-dating:

- Pure Poly-Dating: a state of courting more than one person at a time. One is not trying to score with any one candidate. They want to gather information from their candidates for the sole purpose of making a wise decision about who will be most suitable. This style of dating enables broader options, unlike monogamous dating. Unfortunately, this technique hinders one from giving quality attention to a single candidate, since one must gather information and give time to multiple candidates. If one chooses this form of dating, I recommend taking out no more than two to three candidates at a time.

THIS STYLE OF DATING IS ACCEPTABLE

- Perfidious Poly-Dating (player; juggler; and gold digger): a state of dating more than one person. The person is often in an expressed exclusive relationship, but is sexually involved with other people. The word juggling is derived from the Middle English jogelen (to entertain by performing tricks). He or she is the modern "Player". This style of dating is carried out by a deceptive person that is self-seeking and does not respect the game of dating.

Note: These styles are mixed by the perfidious dater, which to some degree enables him or her to achieve all the developmental and emotional stimuli that someone dating monogamously achieves. They will conduct themselves within a form of monogamy, but reject their responsibility to execute the obligations within it. Paradoxically, those practicing this form of dating can genuinely be "in love" with more than one person.

THIS STYLE OF DATING IS UNACCEPTABLE!

CHAPTER 14

A HOUSE BUILT ON SAND

A man decided to build his house on a sandy beach. The ocean view and sound of the waves were spectacular. One day a storm came, the winds blew and the waves crashed against his house; and, it fell flat.

I told this story to a small group of people and asked them what made the man's house fall. Immediately, most said that it was the storm. Some said that it was the wind, while others said that it was the waves. No one mentioned the foundation upon which his house was built. The man had built his house on sand. Of course, when storms came, the foundation wasn't stable enough for the house to stand.

When storms come in your life, they come to test you. The storm wants to see if you are made of strength or weakness. A weighty concern individuals face, when dating, is the foundation upon which they are building.

HANDLE YOUR BUSINESS

Think of dating as if it is your company. As the business owner, you are the master of that organization; and, the fate of that institution is determined by your decisions. When a successful business owner wants another building, he or she doesn't just purchase, and build on the first site he or she sees; he or she investigates the land and examines other properties around it.

Let's say you have found a suitable piece of land; and, you have secured it. The next step is to design a blue print. Start the sketch in pencil: like all designs, you may have to erase and start over. When designing the blue print for a Stage I relationship, never base it on sex, good looks, money or possessions. These are all shallow and emotional reasons to date. When the sex, good looks and money are gone, what will you have left to hold the relationship together? Your initial reasons for dating will become the foundation of your relationship.

As an individual seeking to date and build a successful Stage I relationship, investigation of original intentions of a candidate is essential. Here are a few things to be mindful of when trying to determine if someone is suitable to date.

1. Be mindful of first impressions. Pay attention to his or her original responses. The original intent of the person can be determined through his or her conversation.

- Is he or she just being polite?
- Is he or she looking to hook-up?
- Is he or she looking for a friend or future spouse?

2. If he or she wants to date, closely examine their associates. Now, picture yourself associating with those same people.

- Are you comfortable with how they communicate?
- Do you feel secure around them and with their social decisions?
- Are they the sort of people that line up with the character in your personal vision?
- Will you grow into a better person around them?

"Oftentimes we allow unresolved issues to persuade us to run into the arms of those who are not capable or responsible enough to be our void filler. We must carry the weight of our own accountability."

Wanda Summers

Ignoring the warning signs may be the reason our lives take certain turns. It is like the news saying that a severe storm with seventy-five miles per hour winds and waves ten feet high is coming. The water and waves start to rise. Over time, the water starts to sway the house, the roof flies off; but, you still won't leave. Usually, it is our arrogance that prohibits us from accepting the fact that we have to start over. Instead of rebuilding and starting over on a sturdy foundation, we stay, hoping the relationship works out. When you build your relationship on superficiality it will never stand the test of life.

When one has been damaged from previous relationships, he or she must restore his or her own mind. Never expect restoration to come from the next prospect. One's restoration must come from within. In order to have a meaningful and long lasting relationship, there must be certain attributes present, such as:

• OPEN COMMUNICATION: Both parties need to talk to each other, not at each other. Seeking to understand what the other person is trying to say is crucial.

• INTEGRITY: Be faithful and consistent in and out of one another's preferences.

• HONESTY: This entails no hidden agendas, deceit and remaining transparent, even when it hurts. You can always work with the truth.

• FLEXIBILITY/COMPROMISE: Be able to bend a little; so, no solo acts. This journey requires teamwork and being able to share the road. In addition, many people say that relationship is give & take; but, I believe it is "give & receive". You never try to take what others are not willing to freely give to you.

• UNIQUENESS: Everyone is different. We all represent a puzzle that eventually portrays a beautiful masterpiece. Some pieces are small, some are larger; however, learn how to embrace one another for the enhancements that he or she brings into view.

"…I am the master of my fate:

I am the captain of my soul."

William Ernest Henley

If the candidate qualifies and you are comfortable with your decision; then, take things extremely slow. Spend quality time outside of the home. End the evening at a safe hour; and, never put yourself in compromising situations. Remember, you are building an appropriate foundation. Set boundaries and standards at the beginning of the relationship. Know what you will and will not accept; then, make sure that candidates understand your expectations. Once you have completed these basic steps, you are well on your way to building a successful and meaningful relationship, one that is not built on sand.

CHAPTER 15

PRODUCT ADVERTISEMENT

P eople say that presentation is everything. Let's say it is only a fraction of the required qualities that is necessary to sustain a relationship. One may score a Perfect Ten on presentation; but, what happens if one does not possess the qualities being advertised? Once one obtains the interest of a candidate, can he or she make the sale by maintaining his or her attention? Don't get me wrong, presentation can be a "make it or break it" portion; but, it is only the icing on the cake, which leads me to a significant question.

WHAT IS YOUR MARKET STRATEGY?

Are you going to be fabulous, ghetto fabulous or just downright ghetto? Building the appropriate image is delivered in one's speech and conduct. Do you act well-mannered around most people, but become loud and boisterous when your friends are around? What is the lasting impression you want to leave with others that meet you? Like a major company has to build the appropriate image, so should you. Start thinking about the impression you want others to have of you when they hear your name.

It is necessary to refrain from creating negative images. For example, we all know that Sex Commerce is a popular industry. When others incorporate sex within their strategy, I call it Sex Targeting. In the game of dating, this practice is unethical. It can be extremely difficult to compete against others who use Sex Targeting as their game plan. In business, it is called Consumer Targeting when a company aims its products and services at a specific group of consumers. It's like a weight loss commercial. I can hear the persuasive voice of the narrator saying, "Try our FDA approved weight loss pills. Lose 10lbs in a week. No exercise needed." To an overweight person, the attributes of this product are irresistible. Sex Targeting is no different from undercutting in the business world, but it is probably one of the dirtiest forms of undercutting in the game of dating.

In business, consumers are called clients. In the game of dating, I call them candidates. Unfortunately, people are going to undercut you; some may even steal your clients. Conclude that any client willing to settle for the unethical tactics of another is not the right prospect or candidate for you. Instead of doing evil for evil, use it as an opportunity to eliminate that candidate. In the business world, when a consumer is a repeat offender, the company may choose not to do business with him or her anymore. If a business is willing to dismiss a consumer, you should be willing to do the same thing in order to protect your inner qualities. If sex is all a candidate wants; then, there are plenty of others willing to do it. I encourage you not to compete against anyone that is using sex as a market strategy. Anyone who uses sex to obtain or maintain a relationship should expect disappointment and failure to be right around the corner.

DEAL OR DUD

A CNN Health report released on January 4, 2007 stated, that marketers of four weight-control pills have agreed to pay a total of at least $25 million to settle allegations of deceptive advertising. The Federal Trade Commission announced that the four products were Xenadrine EFX, CortiSlim, TrimSpa and One-A-Day Weight Smart. The FTC alleged that the companies' weight-loss and weight-control claims were not supported by evidence.

Where is the evidence that you are who you say you are? When you false advertise, hurt will be waiting at the threshold of your heart. In the consumer world, what do we do when we buy a product that does not do what the company said it would do? We return it, exchange it, or throw it away. All these options are forms of breaking up with the product we once thought would be beneficial for us.

Don't be surprised or upset when a candidate breaks up with you. It is only a matter of time before they realize you do not possess the qualities you have been advertising. Instead of getting a DEAL, they believe that they have gotten a DUD.

REJECTION

Accept rejection as a significant part of the game. Rejection can come in various forms. It is like someone who doesn't respond to your calls after a date or someone that says, "We should just be friends". Keep things in perspective, if you are on the receiving end of rejection. An Independent Insurance Agent never expects to get every sale. Instead, they pitch their product, understanding that they will be rejected by many before they get a sale. Being rejected can hurt; and, oftentimes, it is embarrassing. When you are rejected, face the reality of that dismissal. Move on, knowing that you are going to make a sale or acquire a beneficial product.

QUALITY MANAGEMENT

Personal empowerment is essential to building and maintaining inner qualities. Going to school, reading books, listening to self-help audios and getting sound advice are all acceptable methods for building knowledge, good judgment and self esteem.

"People often say that this person or that person has not yet found himself. But the self is not something one finds, it is something one creates."

Thomas Szasz

I do not believe that one must create the entire self; but, this quote holds true for areas in our lives as business owners, students, or companions. Within the game of dating, what makes someone a better candidate than all the others? In the Army, they have a saying, "Be All You Can Be." Most would probably say this means to become the best person you can be. This is a veritable slogan for the Army because in order to be the greatest military force, the soldiers must believe that they are the greatest. Being all you can be also means taking every opportunity to enhance yourself. Are you striving for greatness or are you content being the person others settle for? If the latter is your current lot, I challenge you to "Be All You Can Be."

CHAPTER 16

ESTABLISH BOUNDARIES

In this section, we will discuss various elements to help you further develop your own personalized "dating system". Within your dating system, you must adopt rules and restrictions. The development of a dating system will restrict you from dating the same as everyone else. Your rules and restrictions must be tailored for your personal life, since what works for others may not work for you.

Life Coach Cheryl Richardson is the New York Times bestselling author of several books including "Stand Up for Your Life". She believes that creating stronger boundaries is the number one way for most people to improve their lives with three easy steps. We are going to use those steps as an outline to help us create dating boundaries.

STEP 1: SELF-AWARENESS

Cheryl Richardson says, "The first step in learning to set boundaries is self-awareness. For example, "pay attention when you feel that uncomfortable knot in your stomach, or that I feel like crying moment. Identifying where you need more space, self-respect or personal power are the first steps." She is unquestionably right. Although this book is about dating, the principles we're discussing are applicable to all areas of one's personal life. Before we move on, I encourage you to complete Richardson's personal assessment (see below).

1. Write out a list of things people may not do to or around you.

2. Make a list of things you feel you have the right to ask of someone (e.g. I have the right to ask for privacy, more information before making a decision, and quiet time to myself)

3. Make a list of things that are O.K. to do in order to protect your

energy and time (e.g. It is okay if I choose to turn the ringer off on my phone, take my time returning calls or e-mails, change my mind about something I said I would do, cancel a commitment when I'm not feeling well, or reserve a place in my home that is off-limits to others)

STEP 2: SET YOUR BOUNDARIES AND LEARN TO SET BOUNDARIES WITH OTHERS

Richardson encourages us to start setting simple, but firm boundaries with a graceful or neutral tone. If necessary, find support from a friend or family member before and after each boundary conversation. Initially, it is very important to vent any strong emotions with the person you are dating, before you have your boundary conversation. Talk about your concerns and discomforts. Ask the person you are dating to respect all your present and future personal boundaries; then, move into setting boundaries. Below are some scripts you can use to help you set boundaries for various scenarios.

1.   To back out of a date: "I know I agreed to go out this particular day, but after reviewing my schedule, I now realize that I won't be able to give you my best attention. I'd like to reschedule our date night.

2.   To buy yourself time when making tough decisions: "I need time to think about it, I have a policy of not making decisions right away."

3.   To set boundaries with a person you're dating who requests to borrow money: "I won't be lending you money anymore. I care for you; but, you need to take responsibility for your own finances."

Loaning money of any substantial amount is not encouraged while dating. Since I discourage loaning money while dating, I felt it was important to place emphasis on this topic. This boundary ties directly into the personal economy concept. One may say, "What does my money have anything to do with dating?" Well, there are certain risk factors that must be considered.

- What if the money cannot be returned within the established time frame? Will it strain the relationship?
- What if the money is not returned at all?
- What if the relationship does not last long term and the loan has not been repaid?

If you decide to loan money to someone you are dating, I recommend having the agreement solidified in writing. On the next page I have provided you with a sample to use as a formal loan agreement. It is a shame; but, you would be surprised how often these issues end up in court, or go unresolved.

You may consider it trivial; but, this is an example of healthy standards and maintaining boundaries. Anyone who has been on either side of this issue will appreciate this standard. When loaning money, you never give your bill money, savings, or investment funds. How would it look if you loaned, say, your rent money? What happens if the borrower cannot get the money back to you in time? Ironically, the borrower pays their bills; but, you're left not having enough to meet your monetary needs.

(see next page for Loan Agreement Sample)

PERSONAL LOAN AGREEMENT

This agreement is made January 3, 2012 by and between

JANE DOE
111 State St.
Jersey City, New Jersey
(Herein & after referred to as the "Lender")

&

JOHN DOE
222 Elm St.
Newark, New Jersey
(Herein & after referred to as the "Borrower")

WHEREAS, the borrower wishes to borrow from the Lender, and the Lender agrees to lend to the borrower [Seven Hundred Dollars] $700.00

Repayment: Borrower will pay back in the following manner. Borrower will repay the amount of in Seven (7) equal continuous monthly installments of $100.00 each on the 15" of each month starting February 15, 2012.

Prepayment: Borrower has the right to pay back the entire amount at any time.

Don't forget
to sign the
dotted line.

_____
Signature of Lender

_____
Signature of Borrower

4.   To set a boundary with a person you're dating who wants to borrow your car: "I won't be lending you my car anymore. I care for you; but, you need to take more responsibility for your own transportation."

5.   To set a boundary with a person you're dating who always needs a ride: "I won't be picking you up as much anymore. I care for you; but, it is becoming too much of a personal burden for me."

Richardson says, "When setting boundaries, there is no need to defend, debate, or over-explain your feelings. Be firm, and direct. When faced with resistance, repeat your statement or request. Back up your boundary with action. If you give in, you invite people to ignore your needs."

STEP 3: STRENGTHEN YOUR INTERNAL BOUNDARIES

Richardson believes that we neglect to stand up for what is right for ourselves. She says, "One of the reasons people take things personally is because they have weak internal boundaries. An internal boundary is like an invisible shield that prevents you from taking in a comment without objectively evaluating it first. For example, when someone accuses you of being selfish, stop and consider the statement before taking it in. When you use this internal shield, especially with people who can be difficult to handle, it gives you time to ask yourself questions like, how much of this is a projection from the accuser? How much of this is true about me? What do I need to do (if anything) to regain my personal power or stand up for myself?"

These are immensely powerful principles. The first two steps are worthless without internal strength. When one lacks inner strength, he or she is like a parent who cannot control his or her children, or a child who is unable to stand up to the playground bully. Maintaining boundaries for oneself is as essential as establishing them for others. If you are unable to live by your personal boundaries; then, don't expect others to respect the boundaries you set for them.

"Your personal boundaries protect the inner core of your identity and your right to choices."

Gerard Manley Hopkins

Chapter 17

T.M.I.
"Over Sharing"

"Everybody knows the pressure of a first date: Searching for that perfect outfit. Hunting for ways to be engaging. Dissecting each detail when it's over... Dating can make even the most confident person lose his cool."

Kelly Starling

While dining at a local restaurant, I couldn't help but overhear the conversation of the other couple beside my table. I assumed it was their first date because the man introduced himself as Jacob, and the lady introduced herself as Emily. A waiter came to their table; and, they ordered their drinks. After about ten minutes, I overheard Jacob say, "Yeah, my plan is to get married, and start a family right away. I also want five kids. Do you think your uterus can handle five kids?" My colleagues and I looked at each other in complete shock. We all looked at Emily, who appeared very uncomfortable. We expected a drink in the face; but, to our surprise, she reluctantly entertained him. I even heard him ask her about her favorite sex positions. Needless to say, that date did not last long.

Jacob made a fatal rookie mistake. He did not allow Emily enough time to get to know him or become comfortable around him. Instead, he spilled his guts about his requirements and made some crass comments for a first, second or even third date.

"Blurting out too much information, or TMI, is something we're becoming more and more comfortable with, some psychologists say. "We obsess over the mundane details of celebrities' lives and are eager to tell our own stories on blogs and Flickr accounts; and, often, all that online openness seeps into everyday conversations", says Melissa Dahl, Health

Writer for MSNBC.

Breaking the ice is one thing; but, how far is too far when sharing information? There is a term I picked up called "Over Sharing". Over sharing is providing too much personal information too soon. Sometimes candidates feel they can handle certain information. Too much information too soon can cause anyone to second guess their interest. I once heard a guy say, "I was really into her before she told me how many guys she slept with." I later found out that he requested that information. Although he asked, he could not handle it so early in the courtship.

There are tons of ways to promote awareness for a candidate without showing them your party and binge drinking photos. Sometimes people will use the information we share to exploit us. Telling candidates about current or prior weaknesses can influence them to tempt you. Don't think it strange when a candidate tries to get you into bed on the second date, especially, after you told him or her that you have successfully overcome your sex addiction a mere two months ago. Many people date because they seek after vulnerabilities within others. Their goal is to misuse others; so, don't give them any room in your heart.

Within that introductory stage, we should remain somewhat reserved until we see significant progress. We never know how long the courtship will last. If you over share, you risk your business getting into the hands of someone who will misuse that information. Although you may be proud of your progress or excited about overcoming certain struggles, you shouldn't share everything.

CHAPTER 18

SPACE & SECURITY

UPDATE YOUR STATUS

Shakiba: "Females are soooo insecure! I'm in the bar last night and this chick gets mad 'cause I'm talking to MY homeboy...taps me [on the shoulder] talking about that's her man... LITTLE GIRL, IF YOU DON'T GET YOUR INSECURE SELF OUT MY FACE! I told her to chill out...females! I CANT STAND THEM! People get over it. Your other half CAN HAVE FRIENDS OF THE OPPOSITE SEX!" - March 16, 2011

India: Some females just don't see it like that.

Shakiba: Girl, ain't that the truth.

Joy: So why was her issue with you? You should have told her to talk to her "man." lol

Connie: I would have tapped her back and been like AND!!!

Shakiba: @Connie – lol. Girl, these females today are out of control

Shakiba: @Joy - Chicks don't think...I been there, done that and it's for the birds...I'm too grown for that...

Joy: Right... did he say anything to her?

Shakiba: I'm not sure...but when I woke up this morning, I had a missed call from him; but, it's all good. He's still my homie...

Shakiba received fourteen "likes" after posting her thoughts on Facebook. Personally, I thought she should have received more. I felt that her initial response concerning the matter was reasonable. While dating, you have to understand that your significant other had friends of the opposite sex before you came along. It is not fair for either of you to ask the other to give those friendships up, especially while dating. I am not saying that you should put up with the inappropriateness of your significant other's associates, by any means; but, I believe that trust must be extended to whomever you are courting. Too often we see the crazy girlfriend or boyfriend standing at a distance, watching their significant other's every move. The realm of emotional security is what you choose it to be and how you see the world around you. Jealousy, in itself, is not a bad thing; and, it is natural to protect anything you perceive as belonging to you. Everyone experiences levels of jealousy. Jealousy is no different than any other emotion we feel; but, unfortunately, it is stereotyped as being "bad". Everyone is familiar with the emotion of anger. Is anger bad? Anger is not bad. It is our actions that determine whether or not an emotion is good or bad.

I believe we have two types of jealousy emotions that I call Guardian Jealousy & Stalker Jealousy. One will always be more dominant than the other based on the maturity and discipline of the individual. Everyone has the potential to be the great protector or the crazy stalker. It's all determined by how well a person manages his or her behavior when he or she feels either jealousy type.

Positive or Guardian Jealousy resides within the realm of being emotionally secure. It is that emotional security that is seen in mature and confident individuals. My friend Michael and his wife Stephanie have been married over ten years; and, both possess this maturity. Michael's wife has this thing for muscular men in uniform. Whenever one catches her eye, she has Michael take a picture of her posing with the guy. Most people would feel insecurity rise in them like a blazing fire; but, it doesn't bother Michael. He snaps the pictures; and, they carry on with their day. The guardian character must be balanced by confidence. Michael believes his wife is trustworthy and would not intentionally harm, disrespect or hurt him. Michael's emotional security through trusting his wife allows him to feel freedom, where the insecure person feels bound or threatened. Michael's guardian character kicks into gear when he observes something that threatens the safety of his spouse. If you want to see how much that special person cares for you, watch how jealousy rises within them to protect you physically and emotionally.

Negative or Stalker Jealousy is an indication of emotional instability. If someone lacks confidence and trust, they will never feel secure when their significant other is around the opposite sex. This is the jealousy that influences people to act irrationally.

"Jealousy in romance is like salt in food. A little can enhance the savor, but too much can spoil the pleasure and, under certain circumstances, can be life-threatening."

Maya Angelou

Insecurity can become a major stumbling block, if one's behavior is not managed correctly. For the person who often feels that unhealthy jealousy, he or she must take control of his or her emotions; otherwise, it will contribute to the destruction of his or her relationships. Understand that people do not have to put up with irrational behavior.

When identifying when and why you feel jealousy, ask yourself some questions like:

1. Do I trust the person I am dating? (rate 1-10)

   a. If your answer is less than 10, write your number down and move to question 2.

2. Is this trust issue due to hurt from the current relationship or a previous relationship?

   a. If yes to either case, write a short 2-3 sentence description detailing what happened and why you think you have trust issues in your current relationship.

3. Do you demonstrate signs of an Overly Possessive Person (OPP)?

HERE ARE SOME SIGNS THAT YOU MAY BE AN OPP:

1. You feel insecure while your significant other gives his or her attention to almost anything other than you, such as his or her family, friends or associates

2. You have to be in constant communication with the person you are dating

3. You become offended if you don't get an immediate response when trying to contact the person you are dating

DATING VIOLATION #25

Absolutely and under no circumstance, should you call back to back unless it is some sort of MEDICAL or FAMILY emergency. If there is a medical emergency call 911 first.

Why: These actions are typically seen as disrespectful, immature or clingy.

You must acknowledge and address insecurities before you can ever expect to have a successful Stage I relationship. OPP's induce fear and emotional bondage within relationships. If this is you, be truthful with yourself. Confess it to someone you trust, who will give you proper advice. Counselors or clergy are great sources to utilize as emotional outlets.

Once you identify these areas of insecurity, discuss your issues with the person you are dating. Make the person aware of that particular area of weakness in your life. Subsequently, he or she will typically have more patience with you while you begin a routine of properly managing your emotions and correcting irrational behaviors. Additionally, try couples counseling. Counseling is not only for struggling married couples. It's never too early for counseling, if you want a successful relationship; but, don't expect a candidate to put up with your negative behavior just because you confess certain weaknesses. Confess it, then work on improving yourself.

As the courtship becomes more serious, give that person space by maintaining boundaries. Typically, in that butterfly stage of dating, each person wants to constantly be around one another. This is nice in the beginning; but, when the butterflies fly away, somebody is going to feel smothered. If either party starts to feel stifled, initiate a mutual agreement that the both of you are going to start spending more time alone and with family and friends, apart from one another. This preserves the relationship. As Eleanor Roosevelt said, "Absence makes the heart grow fonder."

FIND PEACE IN SECURITY

When you are emotionally secure, you understand that you and your significant other will always be attracted to other people. The key is acknowledging those attractions in a healthy manner. Revelations of insecurity is not a bad thing. Flares of negative jealousy are good because they help you identify where improvement is needed. When you assume your responsibility for building internal security and trust, things like that won't bother you as much over time.

During a Stage I couple's meeting, I advised a young couple named

Isaac and Suzanne. Immediately, Suzanne says, "We have some trust issues." Shortly after the meeting started, their conversation began to escalate. I allowed it so that they would reveal their private conduct and true feelings during our meeting. As I listened to their debate, Isaac yells, "I'm a guy; and, I'm attracted to other women too. It's not that big of a deal." Then Suzanne says, "Not when you're in a relationship!" As I de-escalated the conversation, I sat back in my chair and took a deep breath.

I told Isaac to stand up and go look out of the window at a garden nearby. With a puzzled look on his face, he obeyed. All within the ear shot of Isaac, I said, "Suzanne, I have a few questions for you, but you may only reply with yes or no." She agreed. I asked her, "Has Isaac ever been unfaithful? She said, "No." I then asked, "Would you prefer for Isaac to be attracted to the same sex?" She said, "No." Thirdly, I asked, "Are there other people you know or have seen on television that you are attracted to?" Hesitantly, she replied, "Yes." Her head sunk into her chest; then, she looked up at me smiling and I smiled back. I knew she understood. I went on to tell her that, as long as Isaac is breathing, he will always be attracted to other women. I told Suzanne that her frustration with Isaac was a little unfair. I informed her that holding Isaac to such an unrealistic standard was creating some of the problems in their relationship. I said to her, "I'm not giving Isaac the okay to gawk at other women or make crude comments; but, if he does something that arouses insecurity, it is your responsibility to dissect it, dispel it or converse with Isaac about it."

No one wants to be with anyone who is outrageously insecure or overly possessive. Naturally, we gravitate toward those who exude confidence, boldness and assertiveness. If you plan on having a successful relationship, these are characteristics that you must possess.

CHAPTER 19
TAKE IT SLOW

A couple of months ago, Melvin Ness changed his relationship status from "In a relationship with Erica Swanson" to "Single". Now, he is "In a relationship with Jessica Pearson." Five months ago, he was "In a relationship with Rita Nelson." In the past seven months, Melvin has been in three different relationships; and, within a one year span, he has been in five different relationships.

A person like Melvin feels like he always has to be in a relationship. As soon as his relationship ends, he immediately pursues another. Those like Melvin, never give themselves time to be uniquely single and emotionally whole. They often rush, engaging in what's not appropriate for a Stage I relationship. Those who operate successfully understand that patience is most often the game winner. Joan Didion said, "Time is the school in which we learn." Time is crucial because it forces others to expose their true personality. Over time, people start to relax around you. After about six months, they no longer ask if they can go into the refrigerator, they just do it. After about nine months, they stop opening doors, buying flowers and whispering sweet nothings in your ear. Before you know it, they've got their feet on the coffee table and are asking for a key to your apartment. During a side bar in a Psychology course I took in college, my professor, who was in his early 60's said, "Taking your time protects you before things get too deep and go too far. It generally takes about eight to twelve months to truly get to know a person; or, is it eight to twelve months before they show you their true colors."

WHEN SHOULD I DATE AGAIN?

In an interview with Laura J. Bagby, CBN.com Sr. Producer, Jason B. Illian was asked this question: How long, after you have broken up, should you start dating again? Some people just jump into the next relationship. Others wait years. Is there a process that you go through? Jason responded by saying,

"I refer to it as "walking back to the castle." When you ride off into the distance with somebody, the longer you ride, the farther away from the castle you are going to be. The problem is that when you break up, you need to go back to the castle to start the process all over again. For some of us, it is going to take longer than others because...the longer you have been in a relationship, the more time you are going to need to spend time "walking back to the castle." A lot of people continue getting into the bad habit of the same broken relationships over and over. They never take the time to learn. They jump from one relationship to another; and, that's not healthy. So, if people would take just the minimal amount of time to walk back to the castle and take time to evaluate...they will see where they made the mistakes and they will be less likely to step into the same pot holes again."

THE SIX MONTH RULE

Dr. Kevin A. Williams recommends what I call his Six Month Rule. After a public or private break up, you take a minimum of six months to recover. This time is intended for focusing on self betterment and getting over previous relationships. After a break up, have you ever found yourself thinking about that person and reflecting on your experiences with them? Typically, when we get out of a relationship, we dive head first into a different one. Many of us do this because we dislike singleness or we assume it will help us get over an Ex. Time spent not dating increases emotional sobriety; and, it helps us think clearer. The Six Month Rule will keep you safe from irrational decision making.

Say, three months after a major break up, you realize you still want to be with that person. You get back together; but, during the break up, you had a brief affair with someone else. Most break ups aren't the finale. The term "breaking-up" has become an overused and abused term. Oftentimes, we use it as a form of intimidation or a method to escape commitment. Now you have to tell your significant other you had an affair and risk losing them for good; but, if you follow the Six Month Rule, you can avoid this problem. The typical excuse sounds something like, "We were broken-up", but that is not a reasonable justification. Do you see how disengaging all relationship dynamics during the first six months can help you? Getting out of one relationship, then jumping into another is no different from someone waking up with a hangover, but reaching for the Miller Light because their mouth is dry.

"Going [too] fast creates 'false intimacy' which leads to getting into the wrong relationship."

Sevin Philips
Relationship Counseling Center

Chapter 20
Carry On Baggage

Latia: "**It's terrible when you've had a sour relationship in the past and you still carry that bitterness into what could be a potentially sweet future, right? So, is it wrong to use precaution and ask questions when you hear or see something that looks similar to what you have already seen and heard? I say it's ok to ask! But then it comes off as having trust issues! What do y'all think? SN: I'm enjoying being single!!" – Aug. 23, 2011

Jesse: "I think it's ok."

Nathan: Yeah. Questions are good.

On my very first airline travelling experience, I was bombarded with all these rules and regulations concerning what I could and could not bring on the airplane. I thought to myself this is ridiculous, but considering the historical issues surrounding flights, I quickly adjusted my attitude. I was informed that in order to keep the passenger compartment uncluttered and safe, airlines place rules and size limits on the luggage that each traveler can carry on the plane. The primary rule is that bags must be small enough to store below your seat or in the overhead compartment. Currently, the basic rule is that carry-on baggage must be no taller than a certain height and width, and no deeper than about 9 inches. In many cases, you will also have to contend with limits on weight.

I thought to myself, "Why don't we adhere to some of the same rules pertaining to people in our lives?" It could be friends, family, associates; but, more importantly, the people we date. Why do we allow people to come into our lives with junk and baggage from past experiences and relationships? They enter our lives and dump all of their issues on us, but expect a smooth and comfortable flight. It is essential to identify whether we are accepting baggage or if we are the ones carrying the baggage from one relationship to the next. Baggage is something that takes up space and adds more weight to an already heavy load. Baggage in relationships can be psychosomatic, economical or external.

PSYCHOSOMATIC BAGGAGE

HURT EXPECTANCY

This person is abnormally paranoid of being hurt. Instead of going on with life, they wait to be hurt by others. They are like people who pick on themselves before others have the chance. People who spend time waiting to be hurt are often less productive and have a difficult time trusting others. Success in a relationship is unlikely because their baggage weighs too heavy on the other person.

FAMILY DEPENDENCY

Oftentimes, dating a person with deep rooted family reliance can be extremely difficult, especially when parents or other family members don't want that person to grow up. To some degree, while in a Stage I relationship, this baggage should be expected. Progression beyond dating a candidate that has a high volume of unstable family matters is not recommended. Give the candidate time to learn how to detach and prioritize family problems. Besides, who wants to hear another person nag about their family drama all the time? Dating a candidate who is easily drawn into family drama can be difficult, especially when those issues find their way to your front door. Being a supportive significant other is one thing, but getting dragged into a heap of family drama, is not where you want to be.

OLD BAGGAGE

This baggage is necessary and should be expected. It is necessary because we have to remember the bad things that happened in the past, so that we can have a genuine appreciation for the good things in the present and future. One day a man's wife was washing dishes in the kitchen. When her husband got home from work, he decided that he would prank his wife by jumping out and scaring her. No sooner than he jumped out, his wife grabbed a kitchen knife. She leaped on top of him and proceeded to kill him. The husband yelled to his wife to stop, but she was so enraged. It was like she couldn't hear him. A short time later, during a counseling session, the husband expressed that he was not sure if he wanted to continue with the marriage. He said the experience led him to believe that she was crazy and he feared for his life. The counselor asked the man's wife why she responded that way toward her husband. The wife said, "Before my husband and I got married, I was raped. The rapist, whom I knew, entered my home the same exact way. He snuck up behind me, beat me, and then raped me." That was her husband's first time hearing that story. Baggage should never be stuffed in a suitcase and pushed to the back of the closet. At some point, baggage has to be checked and approved. If it cannot be approved; then, it must be thrown out before it destroys the relationship. In the case of this husband and wife, I would have encouraged them to work through this new information. In the case of people dating, I urge those carrying baggage to be brutally honest. It is vital to address damaging issues before going into a serious relationship.

ECONOMICAL BAGGAGE

Bad Credit History

Low credit indicates to lenders that you are a high-risk borrower, and they may not be willing to lend you money for things like business endeavors, home loans, or car loans. Poor credit indicates two things about a person: He or she had some uncontrollable circumstances (e.g. lose of employment) or he or she is a person who lacks discipline (e.g. does not pay bills on time).

Excessive Debt

The side effect of having excessive debt is tremendous. Purchasing certain things will give you an initial feeling of bliss from ownership, but the maintenance can be overwhelming. Now that dream home or car is a burden because all of your money is going into retention and maintenance. Generally, those with excessive debts have overextended themselves. Quality educations are great, but why are students accumulating debt loans equivalent to middle class mortgages? Many students are coming out of school with minimum wage pockets, but have acquired student loan debt that is equivalent to average mortgage loans. If you are a person with little to no debt; then, the debt of a candidate must be considered.

Unemployment

Regardless of the reasons for unemployment, a man must be able to take care and provide for his woman and a woman must be able to support her man. If a person has no income, how can he or she support you when you are in need? You may say, "Their love is all I need", but consider this: If one will not work now, he or she is even less likely to work heartily when the relationship gets more serious. When dealing with the unemployed candidate, it is more beneficial to wait until he or she gets a stable stream of income.

CHILD SUPPORT

Honor is extended to those that reliably pay their child support; but, you must acknowledge that the person paying child support is going to be doing this at least until the child becomes a legal adult. Can you handle that? Can you handle the fact that income is going out of your home into another? Some may say, this thought process is shallow, but it is not shallow. It is honest and realistic. If people took more time to weigh their options, they would not have wasted the energy, time and money during previous relationships.

EXTERNAL BAGGAGE

This baggage comes from others, maybe an Ex whose aim is to induce some level of vexation in the life of the other person. It could be because they are joint owners of a business, joint property owners or have a child together. Whatever the reasons are, he or she is out to get the other person.

Management of baggage is something that must be conquered before one is ready to date. Dating a person with excessive baggage is always a hassle. Don't get me wrong, everyone has some form of baggage, but it must be properly managed in order to support longevity in relationships.

CHAPTER 21

THE SOCIAL NETWORK
"DIGNITY & RESPECT"

Our common use of social media is out of control. Consider the famed civil rights leaders like, Levi Coffin, Samuel Chapman Armstrong, Gordon Hirabayashi, Harriett Tubman, Rosa Parks, John Brown, Susan B. Anthony, Dr. Martin Luther King Jr., and Bishop Frank McDaniel Williams. If they could read and observe the activity of our social media accounts, would they be proud or ashamed of us? Some hid slaves. All fought against bigotry, held their ground against discriminatory injustice and/or preached equality in the face of harm and threats against their lives. The same social equalities, respect and common courtesies they fought for and many died for, are liberally disregarded without a moment's thought. Sadly, it has become customary to degrade others to make ourselves feel better.

"Men best show their character in trifles, where they are not on their guard. It is in the simplest habits, that we often see the boundless egotism which pays no regard to the feelings of others and denies nothing to itself."

Arthur Schopenhauer

The great civil rights pioneers did not fight against discrimination and injustice for us to ignorantly feud and humiliate ourselves via social media. Everyone should conduct themselves with dignity, sophistication and respect for others. So how dare we debase ourselves to Facebook, MySpace and Twitter fights? What makes you think it is acceptable to battle and war on social media sites and post lewd comments and inappropriate photography? Truth be told, it does not matter what our friends and associates think is acceptable. What matters at the end of one's life is that they held on to integrity. Where is our self-respect and where has our modesty gone? Many people say that social media, like Facebook, has destroyed relationships, but that is not true. It is the misuse of social media that has destroyed relationships.

Instead of using these magnificent platforms for the enormous potential they possess, like promoting a business, sustaining contact with associates or even maintaining a long distance relationship, we use them for blasting others to the world and venting all our personal problems.

UPDATE YOUR STATUS

Dominique: Facebook should have a limit on how many times you can change your relationship status. After three changes, it should default to Unstable. – Oct. 22, 2011

Cathy: "LOL...LMBO"

One of my pet peeves concerning social media is inconsistent relationship status changes. Does everyone need to know your relationship status changes every month? A couple of years ago, I monitored the relationship status changes on an associate's Facebook account. Over a period of several months, she had at least eight status changes, averaging one status change per month:

On May 3, 2010 she was "In a relationship with ...

June 18, 2010, she was Single again.

June 29, 2010 she was "In a relationship with ...

August 16, 2010, she was Single again.

September 3, 2010 she was "In a relationship with ...

September 25, 2010, she was Single again.

October 20, 2010 she was ENGAGED, but then she changed her status to "It's Complicated" a couple months later.

SERIOUSLY! First, this seesaw affect is unacceptable and nobody cares. Secondly, nobody needs to know your business and the inconsistencies of your love life. On the other side of the coin, you may be dealing with a person who gets mad; and, out of spite, changes your mutual relationship status. A mutual relationship status is the acceptance of a relationship request via social media. Anytime someone has asked me for advice regarding this issue, I gave them three pieces of advice that you should adopt as well:

1. **YOU CANNOT CONTROL ANYTHING HE OR SHE DOES!**

2. To maintain control over yourself, do not accept any further relationship requests from that person, and demand maturity. If it is understood that you are dating exclusively, that should be enough. It does not have to be published for the world to see, and don't let anyone make you feel otherwise.

3. Adopt the mindset I acquired from my father, an attitude of, "You're either in or out, there's no in between." If he or she has to think about whether or not he or she wants to be with you, rather than remain in limbo, give him or her the courtesy of three days (72 hours) to make up his or her mind and not a minute more.

> a.   During this time you will not initiate any form of contact. Don't remind them or coerce them to make a decision.

> b.   After three days, make the decision for them, "It's over, your 72 hours is up" (Refer to "Breaking Up"). Don't bluff, be that cut and dry. The title of this book is The Game of Dating, not Playing Games with your Heart

Anna: "I'm really getting sick of this IN & OUT bull****. You either with me or you're not, MAKE UP YOUR MIND!!!!!!!!!!!!!! So frustrated.com" – July, 26, 2011

Suzie: "I fee you...men can be so indecisive!"

Lawrence: "Well That's not fair. Women are just as bad, maybe worse"

Ashley: @Lawrence. Yeah, I agree it kind of goes both ways.

Who wants to deal with a wavering significant other? For whatever reasons, he or she wants you today, but doesn't tomorrow. If that is you, decide if you are in or if you are out. If you are dating someone that struggles with deciding whether or not they want to be with you, I say, cut them loose. Be with somebody that wants you all the time.

SOCIAL MEDIA SCANDALS

"I am on here for my mother. She was recently scammed by Anthony Handy. She met him about a month ago on blackpeoplemeet.com. The same pictures and similar stories were on his profile. He gave a story that he is stationed in Afghanistan, but his daughter is in Ghana with the caretaker. He went as far as to have ordered my mother Dominos Pizza one day and sent it to the house. He told her that he had something for her a couple days later. UPS showed up with a flat screen 32" smart TV. She thanked him for the TV. He stated that the TV was for his precious daughter "Matilda". He wanted her to send the TV to a PO Box in Accra Ghana. She told him that she was sending the TV back and that she was through with him. He stated that if she doesn't send $5000 and the TV, he would post the naked pictures that she sent him on Facebook. He later changed it to $3000. Later he said, just send my TV. A couple of days ago we began to get phone calls stating that there were naked photos of my mother on Facebook. They are posted through some girls' page named RITA P. They are also being shared by others. We are struggling to get the photos removed off of Facebook. We have gotten the police involved and we have also shared our story with the local news station. PLEASE be careful when it comes to this man. IF anyone has any tips, or if you know what we can do to help get the photos removed, we would GREATLY APPRECIATE it!"

- Anonymous Publisher

I was a witness to the above situation and it broke my heart when I found out about it. One day, on our way home from church, my wife turns to me and says, "BAE! This guy put up naked pictures of this woman on Facebook! I KNOW HER!" She enlarged one of the photos and showed me her phone. As soon as I saw the photo, my heart sunk in my chest. Vexation gripped my heart tightly. My first thought was, "Wow…that could have been me. I'm guilty of Sexting in the past." Not only that, but I couldn't believe someone would sink so low to embarrass someone else. I asked my wife to report the photos to Facebook as soon as we got home.

Note: Sexting is the sending of sexually explicit photos, images, text messages, or e-mails by using a cell phone or other mobile device.

Some years ago, I use to work with a guy who made it his priority to have sex with as many women as he could. Although I refused, he tenaciously insisted on showing me and other coworkers the revealing photos women often sent him. It seemed like he saved every photo, like they were cherished trophies, serving as proof of his escapades and victory over loose and vulnerable women. He often invited them to come up to the job site, not knowing that most of the men around them had already seen them naked. I could waste time talking about the disagreeable nature of that coworker, but he wouldn't have that kind of ammunition, if the women like the one on Facebook wouldn't readily make it available.

Like many of us, what made her so desperate? What possessed her to send someone naked pictures she barely knew? If the women Sexting my coworker knew he was showing their naked pictures to all of his coworkers, would they have pressed the send button? The next time you go to send a naked picture to your boyfriend or girlfriend, think about those situations.

RECEIVE MY WORDS

When will you choose to mature and conduct yourself with confidence and integrity? Some may read this and say, "Nobody tells me what to do. I'm grown." Will you let your ego get the best of you, influencing you to disregard certain parts in this book? The problem in our paradigms is as soon as one thing is said that does not suit how we feel, we dismiss it as nonsense. It is my desire that we live in individual excellence and not within what's socially accepted. To do this, we must abandon many learned doctrines. These modern social doctrines bleed through our deeds, and they scream, "THIS IS MY TRUE NATURE. REGARDLESS OF WHAT I SAY OR WHAT I ASPIRE TO BE, THIS IS THE REAL ME."

"Let us not say, every man is the architect of his own fortune; but let us say, every man is the architect of his own character."

George Dana Boardman

CHAPTER 22
THE WORD *LOVE*

March of 2011, Richard Simmons rushed his girlfriend, Michelle Prizo, to the hospital after shooting her in the face in a WalMart parking lot. Authorities said that Simmons, who was getting tired of being taken advantage of, said he loved her so much that he could not live without her. He developed a plan to kill himself and his girlfriend. After further investigation, authorities said that the couple left a bar and drove to WalMart, where Simmons shot Prizo once. Officials also said that Prizo then leaned on his shoulder, told him that she loved him and wanted to see her mother. Authorities also reported that Simmons said that she would soon see her father (who is dead) and shot her again.

Love is a verb, and a verb naturally expresses action. Love should always express itself through positive actions. Subsequently, this means that those who commonly express themselves in a violent or abusive manner are not conducting themselves in love. I am convinced that a variety of negative emotions can dilute love. I call them "counter feelings". The dominant counter feeling of love is fear. If counter feelings were people, imagine them as gatekeepers. Those gatekeepers have the ability to let other negative emotions in and out of your heart. If fear is present; then, insecurity is nearby and accompanied by many other negative emotions. Within the confession of Richard Simmons, we are able to see the progression and affect of all these negative emotions. Simmons said that he loved his girlfriend, but any relatively intelligent person can tell that what he calls love really is not love.

I have a theory. I am convinced that the true nature of people is so deeply rooted that even their physiology will not allow them to hide it. It is like a person holding their breath. Eventually the body says, "Hey breathe!" Within the body, there is something called the Automatic Nervous System (ANS). It is part of the peripheral nervous system that acts as the control system for lower levels of consciousness, and controls visceral functions. The ANS affects heart rate, digestion, respirations, salivation, perspiration, pupil dilation, urination, and sexual arousal. Most of its actions are involuntary, such as breathing. Some of these involuntary functions can be influenced (i.e. heart rate, urination and sexual arousal), but they cannot be controlled. When a person is under pressure or stress, a fight-or-flight system activates called the Sympathetic Nervous System (SNS). An example of this stress response is a zebra running from a hungry lion: the heart rate increases, pupils dilate and muscular functions intensify. Many people will present everything they think you want them to be until they are put under pressure. Then, you will see their true colors.

IDENTITY OF LOVE

"Love patiently endures and is kind; Love doesn't get jealous; Love doesn't brag, boast or have an arrogant character. Love does not behave in an offensive manner, is not selfish, is not easily annoyed, and doesn't think the worst of others;"

I Corinthians 13:4-5
THE EXCLUSIVE BIBLE

Too often we use the word love interchangeably with "like" and "sexual attraction". Instead of saying what we truly feel such as, I like you or I'm physically attracted to you, we sum it up with what has seemingly become the overused phrase, I love you. The word love is an extremely powerful word, and I am concerned about our societal misuse of its declaration. Love is not a dinner and a movie. Love is not sexually ambitious acts and it is never abusive. The snippet from the Exclusive Bible gives us a clear perspective into the true characteristics and behavior of love. Identification of love is as easy as identifying the characteristics of happiness, anger, sadness, or depression. All of these characteristics are identified by their behaviors. It is no different than a fruit tree. We know an orange tree because of the fruit it yields, and the same for an apple tree.

Every time we start and continue a new relationship, it goes through a process of construction. The establishment of emotional connection takes time, energy and even finances. If you paid $750,000 to have your home built and the construction company called you two days later saying the home was ready. Would you not be apprehensive and suspicious? I get that same suspicion when I hear people say they are in-love, but they've only been dating a few weeks. As you can imagine, I probably resemble Ebenezer Scrooge, as he walks by saying, "humbug" to anything he thinks is nonsense. My seeming distaste is nothing of the sort, but rather concern.

Let's talk about what differentiates love from other emotions. I am convinced that ninety-five percent of the time what we feel in the beginning is not true love, but a resemblance of love. As discussed in Stages of Development, one immediately falls into the Inebriation Phase after the Incipient Stage. This phase is a very deceptive state because we feel a few emotions simultaneously. Side by side these emotions are indistinguishable, but they are very dissimilar in character and behavior. As stated before, definition is the catalyst to understanding. Now let's separate the meaning of these subsidiary emotions that I identify as affections. When dating, the two initial emotions we feel are fondness and sexual attraction. True love germinates and matures after the relationship has been tested.

1. **Fondness** is the emotion you feel when you simply have a special interest in someone. You care about their safety, enjoy their company and don't want anything bad to happen to them.

2. **Sexual Attraction** is primarily a self-gratifying emotion that focuses on what it can get, often in terms of pleasure. Like a horny dog, it has only one focus: pleasure, pleasure, pleasure and more pleasure.

No one ever notices the little innocent dog coming up to sniff the new person, until he starts humping the person's leg.

When people are attracted to each other they present an image they think is acceptable to the other person. The true character of a person is only revealed over time and when they are under stress. In order for gold to be purified it has to be heated up to its melting point. The stress from the heat causes the impurities to float to the top of gold in its liquid state. The very material that we regard as valuable does not look valuable when it is under stress. Time and circumstances are enough to show one the real character of others, but one has to be sober enough to see it and accept it. Maintaining your standards and boundaries will add additional pressure, in view of the fact that your values may conflict with the impure intentions of others.

An associate named Chloe approached my wife and I about her unsuccessful attempts to maintain relationships with the people she was dating:

Chloe: It seems like I can't keep a man.

Me: What techniques are you using to try and "keep" men?

Chloe: Well, you know... but that's not all of course. I try and do everything a woman is supposed to do.

Me: First, because you post so many status updates on Twitter and Facebook; we're always informed about what's going on in your life. Secondly, we have noticed a trend and it concerns us. It seems like you have a new boyfriend every couple of months. Whenever you get a new beau, you get so excited that you can't help but shout it from the roof tops. Saying things like, "You make me feel so special. I can't wait to see my baby. No one has ever made me feel the way you do. It's been a while since I've been in love." Don't get me wrong, there is absolutely nothing wrong with tweeting or facebooking, but you do it with every new person you are dating. One or both things is happening:

1. **You're addicted to the Inebriation phase.** You start a new relationship; but, when the butterflies fly away, you find a way to get out of that relationship, only to pursue an emotional high that the current relationship is no longer giving you.

2. **You're giving too much**. Along with doing everything a woman is 'suppose' to do, if you are giving up more than you should while dating, the man will likely lose interest. You cannot use your body to keep someone and expect success, it doesn't work that way. If the physical is all he wants, once he has scored, it's time to move on to the next challenge.

I advised her to slow down, evaluate her dating strategies and go back to the basics. Often times, we get into new relationships and dive in too deep. When it is time to come up for air, we panic and ascend too quickly, which causes more damage than the descent. Like a scuba diver, if we ascend too quickly, we risk getting what is called, Decompression Sickness. Ascending too quickly after diving can cause nitrogen to dissolve in the tissues, which forms bubbles. This is also called "The Bends" and can result in symptoms ranging from a mild skin rash to unbearable pain. The deeper and longer the dive, the more severe The Bends can be. Essentially, one can cause more damage trying to get back to the surface than one did diving. Do you understand the logic behind my suggestions for not diving into relationships too quickly, but gradually easing into them? Sometimes, those we are interested in are too shallow. Instead of diving in head first, try diving in feet first. That way, you can assess their depth, and control the intensity of your descent. If things get uncomfortable, you can easily get out, hopefully, with little to no emotional damage.

CHAPTER 23
SELF PROTECT

"Guard your heart with all diligence; for out of it are the issues of life"

Solomon, son of David

This text derives from Hebrew origin. The writer is telling his readers to protect their hearts with every ounce of their being. According to Solomon, within our hearts resides every part of who we are. When you give your heart, you are not only giving an emotion, but rather giving others access to the nucleus of who you are. For that reason, I believe the heart was never purposed for giving away. We often hear people use clichés similar to, "You have my whole heart." How can you guard your heart if you're busy giving it away to every person you fall in love with? In order to guard your heart, you must keep your heart.

I once heard that the heart is like a castle. Its major defense is its massively thick walls, surrounded and protected by a deep moat filled with water. The castle is comprised of two main courts: the outer court and inner court. The only access into the castle is over the drawbridge, and you are responsible for what goes in and out. The inner court is very sensitive and must be vastly protected. As the master of your fortress, you must be careful about who gains access to the various courts of your castle. The inner court is strictly forbidden because it is reserved for the trustworthy. Those who are shady will have to stand outside of the walls of your castle because it's not safe to let everyone in.

RED FLAGS

A component of protecting yourself is being able to see the warning signs when they come. These warning sign are not always life threatening, but they can be emotionally damaging in the long run. So what are some warning signs someone within a Stage I relationship should look for?

- **Lying**: When a person lies regardless of how small it is, this is a warning sign for what you should expect if you allow the relationship to progress. Like the old-school people say, "If you tell lies, you'll steal." Small inconsistencies are just telltale signs of the nature or latent nature of the individual.

- **Not Ready for a Relationship Statements**: Generally what this really means is they don't want to make a commitment to you. Watch out for the person who says this but they're okay having sex. Red Flag! They're playing games. Don't fall for one of the oldest tricks in the book: I'm not ready for a relationship. When someone says that, it is, more often than not, another way for saying, I want an occasional sex buddy.

- **Rudeness to Others:** How the person you are dating treats others is an indication for how that person will treat you once the butterflies fly away.

- **Money Problems**: We often hear that mishandled finances or the lack of money is one of the primary causes for divorce, so why continue to date people you already know have money problems? Remember this, your problems become their problems and their problems become your problems. If you manage your money well, do you want a person who doesn't manage his or her finances with the same integrity as you?

- **Moving too Fast:** I've never fully understood the Love at First Sight Philosophy, how can you truly love someone in the sense of "I'd give my life for you" if you don't know that person? I have seen those same 'Love at First Sight' people get to know the person and after getting to know him or her, they realize they wouldn't want to give their life for that person. Although cute in the beginning, this sort of rapid progression is not healthy.

- **Phone Secrets**: Although I do not advocate cell phone evasion, you should be mindful about the communication your significant other is hiding. If you've only been dating for a short period, it's none of your business.

- **Still Friends with the Exes**: Excessive friendliness with exes is a potential problem because the connection never fully leaves, but it does fade over time. Excessive friendliness is an indication that something may still be going on.

- **Constantly bad talks their Exes**: It is not uncommon for others to vent about bad experiences from past relationships but it is not necessary to bad talk those people. As far as they are willing to go to discredit their Exes, you have to consider if they'll hold a grudge if it doesn't work out with you.

- **Fresh out of a Relationship**: When a person has recently come out of a relationship any new/quick relationship is a rebound one. If a person is fresh out of a relationship, they haven't had time to recover from the previous, if recovery is necessary.

- **Excessive Parental Connection**: It's one thing to be close to your parents but when you let one or both of your parents influence you in every facet of your life, even into adulthood, it is a major problem.

- **Doesn't want to be seen with you in Public**: If they see someone they know or you both know, and they're ready to run, that's a red flag.

- **Out of town dates**: Your significant other usually wants to go on dates outside of the local area where you both reside to avoid running into people you know. The common excuse is that they just want to get out of the city. Generally, it's because they don't want to be seen with you around people they know.

- **Midnight dates**: If midnight is the typical time your significant other wants to go out with you, and it's always the same movie theatre, and restaurants, that's a red flag, especially if he or she is not receptive to going out at different times or to different venues.

What if I don't see the red flags? Whether through slight warning signs or manipulative behavior, most red flags are noticeable. It is what we do when we get the warnings that matters most. When you feel progressive discomforts, you should address your concerns. Oftentimes, we try to avoid red flags. If we continually avoid the warning signs, we will always find ourselves in very destructive circumstances.

CHAPTER 24

LONELINESS

"LONELY VS. ALONE"

Have you ever noticed the woman at the restaurant dining alone? What about the man strolling through the park downtown alone, yet they seem content? Most people feel that in order to have an enjoyable time, one must be accompanied by a companion. If I told you this was not so, would you believe it enough to change? Manny "Pacman" Pacquiao is considered one of the best boxers in the world. During HBO's 24/7, he said, "I feel better when I have a lot of people around." Why is it necessary for one to be accompanied to feel better?

A thesaurus will say, the words alone & loneliness are synonymous, but they have significant dissimilarities. Alone means, you are separate, isolated from others as in, "I want to be alone." Loneliness is characterized by, or causing a depressing feeling of being lonesome or destitute of companionship as in, "I am unhappy when I'm apart from others." Feeling lonely is an emotional state that is often stimulated by insecurity.

Loneliness is like a miserable person who will not leave you alone. When he sees you happy and he is not; he will try his best to make you unhappy. Putting thoughts in your head like, "No one wants you, that's why you're alone." This is the problem with Loneliness, if you allow him to reside within your mind, he will persuade you to make choices that you will regret in the long run. He will have you hanging out with losers, having one night stands, being someone's booty call, abusing drugs, alcohol and bowing down to all sorts of peer pressures to feel accepted or loved. We often associate peer pressure to youth, but adults struggle with it just as much as adolescents. Think about it this way: If you were the Titanic; then, Loneliness is the iceberg that shipwrecks you. It is critical to exercise dominion over Loneliness. I have seen others get into things that were physically and psychologically damaging, all because they gave into the sway of Loneliness. Loneliness drives one to an emotional state of dependency. Sadly, there are many who surrender to the tantalizing words of Loneliness, telling them that they constantly need others around for emotional support or some form of stimulation. I guess it's true, misery does love company.

If you are willing to compromise your peace of mind for a temporary laugh, smile, or evening of pleasure, then there are deeply hidden issues present. These issues should be addressed before you consider getting back into a relationship. Don't get me wrong, I understand the gratification one feels when they're around someone they care for, and consider a suitable match, but they should not lower their standards to be with that person. Never date because you are the only single person among friends and family. First, learn to love yourself. The mind is your exclusive world. Before inviting someone new into your life, conquer your world.

"When you're not making yourself a priority, you will begin to feel neglected in your relationships."

Jarrard Goldsmith

CHAPTER 25
BREAKING UP
"LEARN WHEN TO GET OUT OF THE GAME"

In the card game called Poker, when the wager gets too high, the player will fold. When a player "folds", this means the player quits with the purpose of avoiding substantial losses. Players that quit assume or recognize that they are in over their heads, so they "discard". Discard is a term used when players in Poker lay their cards face down. While dating, it is important to know when it is appropriate to discard or disconnect. Most call this breaking up. I call it knowing when to get out of the game. Breaking up is a term used for disconnecting. Disconnection means to sever, detach or terminate the connection between something. That is exactly what one does when breaking up with someone.

What about people who routinely break up, but later get back together? In my opinion, they never broke up. It was probably due to some frustration or infantile behavior. We just go through the motions. Breaking up requires a full disconnection. The mistake that we often make when breaking up is not wholly disconnecting. In the beginning of the book, I encouraged you to institute certain standards: to know what you will and will not tolerate within any relationship stage. Why fight for someone, when they are cheating, abusive or practicing things that go against your standards? As the relationship progresses, tolerance naturally increases. Although forbearance for inappropriate behavior is not expected for an extended time, a higher level of tolerance is expected when couples ascend to superior relationship stages. What people do to or around you during inferior relationship stages is what they will do, if you progress into a superior stage.

Below I have listed good and bad reasons to break up for all relationship stages (except Stage III). Stage III relationships fall under different standards that may be discussed in a later edition.

BAD REASONS TO BREAK-UP

- WE ARGUE A LOT: What typical relationship doesn't argue? Every relationship will have its fair share of disagreements. To argue means to disagree or to debate. Don't jump ship just because you do not agree on everything. What gives arguing a bad reputation is when people become abusive. The goal is to have healthy disagreements. This requires consideration for the opinion of each person. If his or her point of view aligns with your standard or with what's appropriate; then, there is no need to debate. If push comes to shove, get the input of a neutral party. They must be a couple that is nonjudgmental, trustworthy, and will not take sides. That includes family members, regardless of who they are.

- DOESN'T LIKE EVERYTHING I LIKE: Exhibit maturity by respecting the differences in your significant other. Contribute to each other's interest. Sacrifice by doing certain things he or she likes, even if you hate it.

- FINDS OTHER PEOPLE ATTRACTIVE: Do not allow insecurity to fill your heart, if you catch your significant other admiring the differences in another person. Choose to be confident.

Note: This is an exception to the bad reasons for breaking up. If he or she wants someone else more than you, let them go without a fight. You have more important things to do, than wanting someone that doesn't want you.

- DOESN'T LISTEN TO ME: Just because someone doesn't obey everything you say, does not mean he or she is not suitable for you. It simply means he or she is an individual. If you are not married yet.

Lose that urge to control your significant other. He or she is not your puppet, and don't threaten him or her with breaking up. Be mature.

I once heard that every happy couple has at least one breakup behind them. If you see a couple that seems like they have it all together, it doesn't mean they have always had it all together. Learning how to date is trial and error. You will make many mistakes, but learn from them and improve yourself.

"You can't promise anybody a perfect relationship, but if they're trying that's a good reason for staying."

Jarrard Goldsmith

GOOD REASONS TO BREAK-UP

- ABUSE (physical or emotional): There is no reason to stay in an abusive relationship. A person that loves you will not abuse you.
- CHEATING: If someone cheats while in an inferior relationship stage, they are likely going to do it in a superior stage. The Three Strikes and You're Out Sympathy Rule should not apply to cheaters.
- LYING: Even the smallest lies can grow into larger problems. Lying is an obvious sign of disloyalty.
- MANIPULATIONS: If people can't get you to do what they want, they will use manipulation to influence your decisions. It goes without saying, don't allow people to manipulate you.
- HARMFUL ADDICTIONS & HABITS: If someone is a substance abuser, and they were before you met, don't think for one second about spending your life trying to get him or her clean. You may realize that his or her problem is too severe for you to handle.
- YOU ARE TOO DIFFERENT: People grow apart. Their interest, goals and many other things change. When your standards, values

and ambitions no longer align, maybe it's time to move on.

When I become aware that being with a certain person is not beneficial, what are some steps I can take to get out?

STEP 1 - BREAK UP EITHER FACE TO FACE OR OVER THE PHONE

There is no easy way to break up, but it is important to respect the feelings of the other person. If possible, make it your goal to minimize emotional damage. Unfortunately, most people will still have hurt feelings. We simply don't like rejection. Consider giving the other person an opportunity to ask questions, primarily to understand why you are breaking up with them. Maybe their breath stinks, or they have really bad body odor. Regardless of your reasons for breaking up, be honest and firm. Don't allow it to turn into a negative argument. If it is not working; then, it's just not working. Reiterate the facts, "It's not working. It's no one's fault, and it's just best that we move on." If you choose to break up face to face, location is paramount. Meet at a public place, a populated unfamiliar location. The comfort of a familiar location, will likely lead to that so called final kiss or sex one last time.

STEP 2 - GET YOUR HEART OUT OF THE RELATIONSHIP

Make sure it is your decision and not someone else's if you choose to break up with someone. Don't give any hope of getting back together, after you break up with someone. You will likely have conflicting emotions. That's why distance is critical. If it's over; then, it's over. Communication will trap you in an unsuitable relationship. The more contact, the more opportunity that person has to get back into your life. Forsake your compassion, and cut them off! If you keep going back, you will continue to get the same results. Did you say he can change? Well, you said that the second time he blackened your eye. Did you say she can change? Well, this is the second time she's cheated on you. Face the fact that he or she is a bad apple. He or she is too damaged, and you cannot repair him or her. Save yourself before you try to save someone else. Join a support group of your choice or get an accountability partner after a break up. Choose those who give sound advice, have nonjudgmental people that won't cater to your emotions and listen to them. More importantly, rely on your values.

DATING VIOLATION #19

Holding on to old gifts from past relationships like clothing, shoes, pictures, cards, love letters, Jewelry, etc. is not a good practice. Get rid of anything that reminds you of an Ex, it only keeps you stuck in the past.

STEP 3 - NO CONTACT

Although you may be the one to break up, you need time to heal. Avoid places of likely unplanned encounters. Avoid all forms of contact for as long as you need. Change your number; block them from your social media sites if necessary. Don't sabotage yourself by visiting their Facebook or Twitter account fishing for information or looking at their pictures. No contact helps both parties move on faster.

FACEBOOK QUOTE

"Your past has no business in your future, let it go."

Steven Boulware

Chapter 26
No Games

Although I metaphorically speak of dating as a game, the similitude does not negate one's responsibility to take it seriously. Unlike Monopoly or PlayStation, dating is much more than amusement. With video games, if you make mistakes or a bad move, you can simply start over. If you mess up in a relationship, there is no restart button.

There is a side of the game that I discourage. It is the temptation to act in an evasive, deceitful, manipulative, or trifling manner. Everyone must take responsibility and conduct themselves maturely.

"People don't understand that not only can they make a difference, it's their responsibility to do so."

Florence Robinson

It's easy to get caught up in the common practice or mindset of, "screw you, me first." Deep down inside, most want commitment and faithfulness, even the Player. When he or she finds someone he or she likes, he or she is heartbroken if he or she discovers that person also has someone else on the side. A Player is someone that has an ambiguous state of mind. Players, although unfaithful, desire faithfulness, and even though undeserving, they desire trustworthiness. They are double-minded, resulting in emotional instability. The typical Player has at some point been cheated on by one or more people. Now, they are afraid of commitment. They are double-minded because deep down they want mutual commitment, but their fear persuades them otherwise. On the other hand, once a person gets a taste of that relationship style, it's hard for him or her to go back to a mindset of faithfulness to only one person.

Even if we sympathize with the likely cause for the Player mentality, it still does not negate one's responsibility to faithfulness.

HIT-IT & QUIT-IT

I am relatively certain that you are familiar with the infamous Hit it & Quit It cliché. Some time ago, a friend came to me for advice regarding a relationship he has been in for a while. He wanted advice about how to get out of a Stage I relationship:

Me: Why are you having trouble disconnecting, and what originally attracted you to her?

Friend: Her body. Originally, I wasn't going to talk to her because I knew there was nothing more than that. I'm struggling because every time we break up, I go back because of the sex.

Me: Why did you initiate a relationship knowing that you were only attracted to her body?

Friend: Well, I would see her all the time at church, and would talk about her to my friend. He told me to hit it and get it out of my system. I thought I could get in and out. I knew it was wrong. I knew we weren't right for each other; now I feel trapped. I'm afraid to hurt her, and I know I will. I should've stuck to my principles and did what was right. Now, I have to clean up a mess I've made, all because I listened to unsound advice.

Since my friends' biblical beliefs discourage this behavior, it made it easier to push him toward a more honorable path. I could tell that he was remorseful; so, I immediately reassured him and informed him that it would be a process to disconnect.

Although my friend is what most would consider a "good guy", he used one of the grimiest dating schemes. It is dishonest, deceptive, selfish and downright trifling. There is no excuse that can present this method as an acceptable dating practice. Be honest with yourself. If you are not the faithful type; then, don't express a commitment to anyone. Man-up, woman-up, and be honest with the other person.

Yeah, I know. If it was only that simple, the world would be a better place. Think about it. Maybe we would have less baby daddy/baby mama drama. I have come across dozens of people who knew their motives were erroneous. They knew that they did not have what it took for the relationship to work, but went in anyway. I consider people like this delusional and deceptive by nature. They are people who jump from relationship to relationship, sabotaging it after things become too serious. You know, that friend or family member you expect to have a new beau at the next family reunion, maybe that's you. Unfortunately, when the other person starts to get serious about the relationship, they are eventually left brokenhearted, confused and angry.

That is no different than the Kim Kardashian and Kris Humphries masquerade. Needless to say, what they had never deserved to be called a marriage. Humphries seemingly made many changes and accommodations for their relationship, only to be told he was no longer essential to her life after only three months of so called matrimony. Regardless of her excuses, one has to admit, the whole ordeal was, to a certain extent, stupid. Her methods reflect the attitude of the masses. We vow to be faithful and committed, but bail when it gets difficult. Whether she moved too fast or not, she made a commitment and vowed before witnesses and God. A marriage is like a baby. What is the standard of our culture when women don't want their children? They abort them or give them up for adoption. This standard is the pattern of our society with everything we don't want. Instead of committing, we just give up on it. That's what Kim Kardashian did. She gave her three-month old baby up for adoption.

Hey, I thought this book was about dating? It is, but there has to be commitment and faithfulness even within that. Nowadays, those two standards have become a joke, nothing more than a witticism, or an amusing anecdote. To have success within and become a sophisticated dater, you must change your view of marriage. If marriage is the epitome of all relationship stages; then, our view of marriage will affect how we view subordinate relationship stages.

Section III
Dating Dynamics

In this section, we will discuss and highlight the diversity within relationships. Since no one person is the same, every relationship will be different or diverse in nature. By acknowledging diversity, you will realistically see the dynamic of your relationship among candidates. There are many things that affect our involvement with others. Individually, we must assess the developmental stage and stability of those relationships. It is essential to grasp the reality that what works for others, will not always work for you. Those dating or within superior stages have different motivations. Be mindful that the stability of their relationship will often differ from your own.

CHAPTER 27
AGE GAPS

When dealing with the subject of considerable age differences, I have little to say. I stay away from topics pertaining to why, and whether or not significantly older adults should date younger adults. Besides, everyone is entitled to make their own decisions. Those choices should be respected. I believe it is more relevant to address the statistical outcomes of these relationships and what both parties should be cognizant of while dating.

Consider Estelle and George. They have been dating exclusively for about three years. Estelle is a 23 year old model, and George is a 42 year old businessman. Estelle wants to get married and have children, but George is unenthusiastic about the idea. George has married and divorced twice. Lately, he has been putting a lot of time into his businesses. George often spends 12 hour days at the office, while Estelle spends most of her time waiting for him to come home. For the past two years, Estelle has been living with George. I had an opportunity to eat lunch with and interview the couple. They provided me with a lot of sound advice about this subject. Upon meeting them, I could tell that the relationship had become to some extent overwrought. Estelle was snappy, and George seemed carefree of the outcome of their relationship.

George had grown somewhat uncomfortable with how others viewed his relationship with his much younger companion. Estelle expressed that she wanted to have more fun together and felt she was spending most of her time waiting for George to come home. A few days later, I noticed that their Facebook relationship statuses went from "In a relationship with…" to "Single".

I sent individual messages asking how things were going. Estelle responded an hour later, saying that she just got tired of the monotony of their relationship, and that she was angry that she let him waste so many years of her life. I was more interested in the level of commitment George made to Estelle. I asked her if he had promised to marry her at some point. She said, "No. We've discussed it, but he would always tell me that he wasn't sure if he wanted that at this point in his life. He said he didn't want another failed marriage. He would often say, "Singleness is better than facing divorce, let's just take it slow." He would tell me, "Sweetie, I'll be home at such and such a time." He would come hours later. Overall, he never had time for me." From her initial responses, I considered it wise not to ask any more questions. I chose to thank her and bid her good fortune in her pursuit of happiness.

George responded a few days later saying, "Estelle left me. I came home, and her stuff was gone. It's different not having her here, but I think her decision will benefit both of us. I need someone with more consistency, life experiences and maturity, but unfortunately I prefer dating younger women. Plus, she was moving a little too fast for me."

My reason for sharing the relationship experience of George and Estelle is to give you a glimpse of how their age gap has influenced their relationship. It is believed that wide age differences increase the likelihood of splitting up and generally the much younger partner is likely to be unhappy than in more customary relationships. Older adults have a saying, "Been there, done that; I even have the t-shirt." In other words, what is fun, exciting, and new to the younger person will likely not be as entertaining, intellectually stimulating or as emotionally fulfilling to a much older person. Remember, they have been there and done that.

Older adults that choose to date younger adults must constantly remind themselves that the younger adult has not experienced as much as they have. On the other hand, if one chooses to date an older adult, one must accept that they may not have the same interests. An older adult may hangout and indulge the interest of the younger in the beginning, but after a while, the older companion may want to do things that are much simpler.

Younger adults should avoid dating older adults who are in the midlife crisis stage. They pursue younger adult mates, because it helps them capture a sensation of youthfulness. They want to feel like they still have it. Younger adults bring a sort of rejuvenation to the older companion, a new energy in a sense, and many of them may only want you for that reason. You will find yourself in a dead end relationship, expecting things that are never going to happen. Don't be like Estelle. She devoted three years of her life hoping for something that likely wasn't going to happen. She played herself, because she knew that George didn't have the same interest. Being with an older person requires an unusual level of discipline in comparison to customary dating. Older adults know what they want, which means they are probably set in their ways. If anything, you will likely have to make the most changes in order to meet their standards and expectations.

Older adults should avoid dating younger adults that exhibit lower levels of maturity. As the significantly older individual in the courtship, he or she has a responsibility to look out for his or her best interest. Sometimes the younger companion genuinely doesn't know any better. They will go into the relationship with blind folds on, thinking they can see. Set expectations in the beginning. If your propositions are acknowledged, but ignore, consider disconnecting. They are not ready for the discipline that is required to be with you. Although you tell them marriage is not an option right now, they will likely press the matter. You may inform them that you have to fulfill certain obligations regularly, but they will only demand more of your time. These are all indications that they are not ready for anything beyond a Stage I relationship. More than likely, they will only frustrate you, and in the long run, you will end up pushing them away.

The older adult is expected to have a much higher level of maturity. Let's say this is the case every time. Mature and dependable people usually expect the same qualities in the people they date. Older adults will likely encounter what I consider intellectual and character deficiencies within the younger people they date. Expecting qualities in another, who is just not there, can be frustrating. You will often see the more mature partner encouraging and pressuring the other to increase reliability, responsibility and overall maturity. As stated in the chapter entitled "Suitability", a key component concerning the success with any candidate, regardless of age, is their propensity to fit one another. There must be cohesiveness between both candidates in order for the relationship to have a chance.

Chapter 28
Long Distance Dating

A CCN Travel report entitled, "In Love, Will Travel" by A. Pawlowski stated, "Joe Whitfield catches a flight from St. Louis to Atlanta so often he knows some of the airport gate agents by name. They're convinced he's a business traveler, but work isn't the reason he's shuttling back and forth so urgently between the two cities. Whitfield is on the road for love. Like many people these days, he lives in one part of the country, while his sweetheart, Chandra Thomas, lives in another. They use phones, webcams and online chats to stay in touch as often as possible, but they long for the time when a plane or a car can finally take the distance out of their long-distance relationship -- if only for a while. "We manage it by keeping our eye on the next trip ... knowing there's another trip around the corner and knowing that because we don't have as much time as others, that the trip is going to be full of romance," said Whitfield, who attends law school in St. Louis. "We are always trying to figure out how to see each other," added Thomas, a freelance journalist in Atlanta. It's a familiar scenario for many couples as careers, studies and economic realities keep them from living in the same place. The U.S. Department of State, which sends its workers all over the world, calls such lovers "geographic singles." But long-distance relationships are also big among young people: up to half of college students are dating from afar and as many as three-quarters will be at some point in time, according to a study published last year in the journal Communication Research.

For countless people that study abroad, go on business trips, work jobs and attend universities in different states, Long Distance Dating (LDD) is not a deal breaker anymore. Through technology, distance is no longer an obstacle to love as long as people can call at will, text,

Skype, or chat online. In a study of long distance dating relationships, Carpenter and Knox (1982) found that males are more likely to sustain a relationship if they visit their partner frequently, and if the visits are initiated by the female. Although I do not condone it, their study went on to say that the relationship is sustained, if the male also dated other people during the separation. Next, their study illustrates that only two factors influence females' relationship maintenance: emotional involvement and commitment to the future of the relationship.

For fear of unfaithfulness, LDD can be a scary commitment, but it can work. This fear is typically driven by insecurities and distrust. Whether those who cheat are one mile or 10,000 miles away, cheaters will cheat. There are people that make LDD work, like those who serve in the military, others who have jobs in different states, and college students that go home during the summer. The key is to assess the pros, cons and what one considers deal breakers.

It can be difficult maintaining long distance dating, after one has become accustomed to seeing the other person on a daily basis. Adjusting to life without the presence of someone you care for, can be a tumultuous process. Some people choose not to spend their days pining after their absent significant other. Rather than remain faithful, some agree on an open dating policy, which allows them to also date other people. Some people actually adopt a "Don't Ask, Don't Tell Dating Policy." In other words, if you don't ask, I won't have to tell you about the unfaithful and disloyal escapades I've engage in during your absence. This dating policy is something I'll never condone or encourage. The standard of the immature think that encouraging faithfulness means placing limitations on oneself during the time they can be enjoying life. Contrary to popular social beliefs, faithfulness to one is a safe haven. The principles of faithfulness protect you.

Take marriage as an example, when both people are faithful to one another, many risk like STDs and pregnancies outside of the relationship are nonexistent. If one person is unfaithful, those same risk factors increase significantly. The Center for Disease Control and Prevention estimates that one in four teenagers contract STDs. One in two sexually active people will contract a STD by the age of 25. It is estimated that one in four people have genital herpes. Due to the infection not presenting itself in the usual form of sores or lesions, 90 percent of these people are unaware they have the STD. The symptoms of Gonorrhea, Syphilis, Human Papillomavirus (HPV) and Chlamydia can also be difficult to identify. The scary thing is while many STDs are easy to treat, if identified soon, undiagnosed STDs can lead to severe health complications. That is why I encourage abstinence and faithfulness before marriage and faithfulness within marriage.

It is important to know your personal deal breakers. A deal breaker is a broken promise or something you will not tolerate from a candidate. Take ordinary friendships, for example, we make deals or promises to be faithful, loyal and true to those people, but we sometimes break those promises. When we violate the trust of another, that desecrated expectation is a representation of our broken deal or promise. When deals are broken within courtship, one has to assess whether or not the connection is salvageable. If the connection is salvageable; then, forgiveness must take place, and one must move forward. If you identify that the connection is unsalvageable; then, there should be a disconnection. Depending on the individual, when trust is violated, it can take a matter of days, months, even years before it is regained. Sometimes it is never regained, and that is when each person cuts loose, and moves on.

Everyone has a breaking point, that place where they just cannot take anymore. Whether it is cheating or lying, know your breaking point, no matter the obstacles you face. Understand that LDD does not have to be the determining factor for whether or not you continue dating a candidate. LDD can work, if both people want it to work.

CHAPTER 29
HOOKING UP
"CASUAL SEX AFFAIRS"

H ooking up, also called "casual affairs," is a major dating violation. Let us go over some statistics. According to the Center for Disease Control and Prevention (CDC):

HUMAN IMMUNODEFICIENCY VIRUS (HIV)

A new estimate released November 29, 2011 found that just 28 percent of the 1.2 million people living with HIV in the United States are receiving optimal treatment. Some 20 percent of Americans with HIV are unaware they are infected, making it more likely they will transmit the virus to others. Among those receiving HIV care, about 77 percent achieve a fully suppressed viral load. Just over 75 percent of people diagnosed with HIV are linked to care within four months, but only 50 percent remain in care.

GENITAL HERPES

A national study showed that this infection is exceptionally common in the United States. Nationwide, 16.2%, or about one out of six, people 14 to 49 years of age have genital HSV-2 infection. Genital HSV-2 infection is more common in women (approximately one out of five women 14 to 49 years of age) than in men (about one out of nine men 14 to 49 years of age). Transmission from an infected male to his female partner is more likely than from an infected female to her male partner.

CHLAMYDIA

The most frequently reported bacterial sexually transmitted disease in the United States. In 2009, 1,244,180 Chlamydia infections were reported to CDC from 50 states and the District of Columbia.

GONORRHEA

The CDC estimates that more than 700,000 persons in the U.S. get new gonorrheal infections each year. Less than half of these infections are reported to CDC. In 2009, 301,174 cases of gonorrhea were reported to CDC. Gonorrhea is spread through contact with the penis, vagina, mouth, or anus. Ejaculation does not have to occur for gonorrhea to be transmitted or acquired. Gonorrhea can also be spread from mother to baby during delivery. Any sexually active person can be infected with gonorrhea. In the United States, the highest reported rates of infection are among sexually active teenagers, young adults, and African Americans.

SYPHILIS

In the United States, health officials reported over 36,000 cases in 2006, including 9,756 cases of primary and secondary (P&S) syphilis. In 2006, half of all P&S syphilis cases were reported from 20 counties and 2 cities; and most P&S syphilis cases occurred in persons 20 to 39 years of age. The incidence of P&S syphilis was highest in women 20 to 24 years of age and in men 35 to 39 years of age. Syphilis is passed from person to person through direct contact with a Syphilis sore. Sores occur mainly on the external genitals, vagina, anus, or in the rectum. Sores also can occur on the lips and in the mouth. This disease has increase and has doubled since 2000-2006.

Any sexually active person can be infected with any of these diseases. Many of these diseases can also be spread to the unborn child of a pregnant woman. The greater the number of sexual partners, the greater risk of infection, which is why hooking up is discouraged. Casual affairs may include make-out sessions, or physical stimulation. An affair is an intense amorous relationship, usually of short duration. Affairs can occur within any relationship status. Oftentimes, people simply engage in the act of sex for fun. People that habitually hook up, typically find it extraordinarily difficult to be faithful in monogamous relationships. They have fashioned an internal nature that wars against monogamy.

FACEBOOK QUOTE

"Fast Food Relationships"

"They are convenient, easy to get to, never really satisfying, leaving you wanting something else. In the long run they are unhealthy and end up putting [extra] weight on you…time to switch your diet."

Michael Brice

If you are engaging in casual affairs, beginning a process of purging is recommended. Stopping negative behavior is never an easy task because psychologically and physically you crave the stimulation. Consider how many people have contracted diseases from past relationships. The person who gave it to them is not even in their life anymore. Later, they may even meet "the love of their life" but cannot offer their full potential because of past actions in previous relationships. I am familiar with several married women who seem barren because they contracted certain STD's from earlier relationships. Their husbands have expressed and prepared for children, but unfortunately, those women struggle to get pregnant.

I encourage those who are unmarried to stop such counterproductive behaviors urgently.

There will come a time when you will want a monogamous, long-term relationship. You may already be at that point. A major flaw in the system of hooking up is that while you are busy satisfying your physical cravings, the respectable person that is suitable for you, may be observing you. As that person monitors you, two factors will come into play: He or she will likely see that you are busy with a mate and move on. If you are one that engages in private affairs, you are more likely to cheat because you are not getting what you want from the new person. Take sufficient time to disconnect emotionally from previous sex partners. That suitable person may be a person that values chastity. Since you cannot get sex from him or her, you may be tempted to get it else where or from a previous lover.

FACEBOOK QUOTE

"Are you a Rental or a Mortgage?"

"Some people who rent don't care about the property they have. They let it get run down, beat up, and don't care what it looks like. They use the space until they find something better. They decline a new lease, move out and they're on to the next rental. People, who buy a house, take care of the plumbing, make sure the yard is beautiful…walls are painted, etc. They are proud of their purchase and they make their property their home! Ladies, which one are you, rental or mortgage?!!!"

Alexis Alexander

CHAPTER 30
PLAYING HOUSE
"COHABITATION"

Jamie and Ashley have been together for five years. Both share a joint bank account and are on the same cell phone plan. Jamie works a full time job and pays most of the bills, while Ashley is a full time student and works part time. She has taken on the responsibility for making sure the home is clean and tries to have meals prepared when Jamie gets home after work. Jamie and Ashley share in the responsibilities of the household and agree on most issue except, the timing of marriage. Jamie feels that you have to live with a person and get to know them before you get married. Ashley grew up learning and feels very strongly that you should refrain from living together before marriage. A year ago, they glazed over the issue of marriage after attending the engagement party of a mutual friend who was engaged shortly after a year. After the party, as they approached their car, Jamie turns to Ashley and says:

Jamie: Are you okay?

Ashley: Yeah, why?

Jamie: I know you were probably uncomfortable, because we have dated, this long and I have not asked you to marry me.

Ashley: Well, it was a little uncomfortable, especially being the only one of my friends still not married after five years. But, do not feel pressured to marry me if you do not want to.

I know some ladies are thinking, "Ashley is crazy. I wouldn't put up with that." Before you judge, examine yourself. Regardless of gender, how often do we put ourselves in the position of settling? How often do we lower our standards for the comfort of others? In this situation, and like millions of other relationships, Jamie gets the benefits of marriage without the actual responsibility of entirely committing. Can you blame him? If Ashley is always willing to settle and lower her standards for Jamie, why would he feel an ounce of urgency to make a full commitment? Unbelievably, Jamie is hard working, honest, and he takes very good care of Ashley, but like many people, Jamie likes his cake and ice cream, and he expects to Buy One Get One Free. This is not only about relationships, but it can apply to settling for friends, family, or a business partner.

"People with self-respect exhibit a certain toughness, a kind of moral nerve; they display what was once called character..."

Joan Didion

Regardless of your personal justifications to validate reasons to cohabitate, cohabitation in comparison to legal marriage is only a pacifier. Cohabitation usually refers to an arrangement where two people decide to live together on a long term or permanent basis in an emotionally and/or sexually intimate relationship. The term is in reference to couples who are not married. Though this edition is not about marriage, there must be a distinction. Cohabitation is a temporary fix to an inconclusive decision. Typically, one, or both in the relationship have not agreed to make things official or the couple living together cannot legally marry. Why are we more inclined to move in with a candidate instead of taking our time and doing it the right way?

"In a contemporary study of young children, a researcher offered each child a piece of candy. The children were then told that if they waited for another researcher (who would return in five minutes), they would get two

pieces of candy. The researchers noted each child's choice – get some right now or get even more in a little while. The researchers tracked each child's life all the way into adulthood. They found that the children who waited for the extra candy were far happier and successful throughout their lives."

Each child had an opportunity to receive two pieces of candy. The first offer was 50% of the proposed opportunity, and the second offer was 100%. What caused some children to wait for 100%, while others settled for only 50% of the opportunity? I believe the core difference is maturity. Immaturity causes you to miss out on life-enriching opportunities. Each child was offered the same opportunity, but did not have the maturity to wait. As an adult, one may say, "Oh, five minutes, that is nothing." What if you have to wait five years? In adulthood, you may say I would wait. How many lies have you told saying you were going to do something, but did not?

If our society conducted itself in patience and discipline, there would not be as many single parent households, college dropouts or as many people in waiting rooms scheduled for STD screenings. Many would be much further in life, but instead of going to class on time, studying to enrich our lives, many of us played house. Instead of waiting, now you are visiting Planned Parenthood , or should I say, Unplanned Parenthood. You may say everyone goes through that, but I am inclined to disagree. Some people stay focused and refuse to fall prey to nonsense. Many finish college, maintain good credit, and commit to organizations that benefit their community. Many dedicate their lives to enriching themselves and others. If we would just exercise patience and faith, with the expectation of getting the best for our lives, how much further would we be in our relationships, finances, education and self-esteem?

Dennis Franck, National Director of Single Adult Ministries wrote an essay entitled "No Marriage? No Ring? No Problem!" Many of his facts were gathered from the U. S. Census Bureau. According to his research and historical findings before 1970, cohabitation was called "living in sin" or "shacking up" and it was illegal in every state of the union. Today these two terms have changed to softer verbal expressions such as "living together," and "cohabitation," and currently only seven states (Florida, Michigan, Mississippi, North Carolina, North Dakota, Virginia and West Virginia) have laws making unmarried cohabitation illegal, although they do not enforce it.

Dennis Franck believes there are three chief types of cohabitation:

1. Moving toward a marriage commitment
2. Cohabiting as a temporary alternative
3. Cohabiting as a permanent alternative to marriage

Within his essay, Franck provides a long list of reasons explaining why people chose to live together summarized into one or more of the following:

1. **Anti-marriage sentiments:** Marriage is often felt to be repressive and irrelevant, so many use cohabitation as a deliberate means for an alternative to marriage. They believe it gives them more freedom in the relationship to come and go.

2. **Avoidance:** This is an effort to avoid a future divorce, which is so common in today's society. Oftentimes, watching your peers get married and divorced can really enforce the logic that cohabitation is a much better choice.

3. **Conformity to social pressure:** The excuse, "everyone else is doing it" is often used. Some individuals believe something must be wrong with a person who is not willing to live together.

4. **Convenience**: It is more convenient for two to live together than for one to live alone. Transportation, shopping, and many other issues become easier, as well as the perception that it is easier to give up the relationship if it does not work out. Simply stated, cohabitation is viewed as a convenient way to obtain the advantages of an intimate relationship without the long-term commitment of marriage.

5. **Compatibility**: Living together becomes an endeavor by couples to determine how compatible they are. Many people feel that it is better to move in together to see if they can tolerate the other person's personality long term.

6. **Economics**: Reasonably, cohabiters believe it is cheaper to move in together than to live separately for example, why pay for two apartments?

REALITY CHECK

Of the reasons listed, determine which categories you fall into, and then consider if your reasons are appropriate. When you are filing taxes, you will find a section that tells you to check if you are single or married. If you are a single person, do you check "married" on your tax forms? You do not mark "married" because you could get into legal trouble. If the IRS, which is a vital part of the US fiscal economy, understands the concept of single vs. married, why are so many people marking "single" on their tax forms, but living as if they are married expecting to have a long lasting, meaningful relationship?

According to unmarried.org, statistically over 12 million unmarried partners lived together in over 6 million households in 2007. The number of cohabiting unmarried couples increased by 88% between 1990 and 2007, so it is not ironic that 55% of Americans approve of men and women living together without being married. Fifty percent of different-sex cohabiters marry within five years of moving in together but keep in mind that forty percent break up within that same time, and about ten percent remain in an unmarried relationship for five years or more.

5 out of 10	4 out of 10	1 out of 10
relationships	relationships	relationships
cohabiting will	cohabiting will	cohabiting may
likely marry	FAIL!	never marry

Chapter 31
Bad Apples

Angela has been with the same guy since freshman year of college. She knows that this relationship is unhealthy for her, but she cannot seem to shake it. Eventually, she breaks up with her boyfriend of four years. A few weeks later she starts dating someone from her church named Ron. Angela soon recognizes that Ron is the type of guy who likes to take his time getting to know someone. Every other weekend Ron would take her on a date, simply to get to know her. Ron would even have her home by 10pm, and escort her to the door of her apartment. Occasionally, Ron would bring her lunch, and tell her something positive he thought about her. Angela liked Ron a lot, but the relationship was not moving fast enough for her. After about four months of dating Ron, Angela got a call from her ex-boyfriend begging her to take him back. Angela became torn and confused. Angela reasoned within herself entertaining thoughts like, "Should I get back with my ex or not? I have been with him so long, and I have put so much time into that relationship. Maybe he will change."

Ron decided to surprise Angela with a gift. His plan was to leave a dozen roses at her doorstep with a note. When he arrived, he recognized a vehicle similar to the description she gave of her ex's car, and it was parked beside Angela's car. Ron's red flag went up. Within seconds, he recalled all the negative things Angela said about her Ex. Angela told Ron that the Ex cheated on her numerous times, and gave her Chlamydia, then lied about it. Adding insult to injury, she found out later that he had already been treated for the STD. Ron decided to call Angela, but got no response. Usually Angela responded immediately. The lights were on in her apartment, so he decided to knock on the door, but still, no response. Right before Ron called again his phone started to ring, it was Angela.

Angela: (whispering) What are you doing here?

Ron: I have a surprise for you...why are you whispering?

Angela: You shouldn't have come over today without letting me know.

Ron: Why, what's so different about today than any other day? Is something going on?

Angela's ex-boyfriend: (Right before Angela could respond the Ex takes the phone out of her hand and says to Ron) Angela and I are back together, so your services are no longer needed. (Phone hangs up)

You are probably thinking, poor Ron, but he will be okay. Sure, this experience will sting a little, but he maintained his standards and kept things from getting too serious. His standards saved him from months or possibly years of emotional healing. Ron knows the game very well. He understands that in every bunch of apples, there are going to be some bad ones.

YOU CAN'T CHANGE'M

This topic alone should have its own book. Over and over, we see desperate people, taking deceptive measures to procure and fashion others into who they want them to be. You cannot change whom a person chooses to be, or how they choose to behave. I have observed both genders spend years with people trying to make others be the perfect candidate. While you are putting all that work into creating the perfect man or woman, you are accepting undue stress and anxiety. Why put up with cheating and dishonesty. Do you not deserve better? When will you get some self-respect and draw the line? When will you say, "Enough is enough, I won't tolerate this sort of behavior in anyone."

Lydia: "Some men just don't want a good woman period...I don't have time for their wishy-washy ways...Goodnight people" – Mar. 26, 2011

Latisha: "I know that's right, I definitely agree with you!!"

Randy: "True, but some women are the same even worse!"

Lydia's complaint is likely due to an unhealthy relationship, but what is she getting from her FB friends in response? All I hear is validation and additional blame, but unfortunately, without any solutions. When we get hurt, we often start the blame game. We hardly ever take responsibility for ourselves. Consider how you could have avoided harmful situations or how you could have contributed to personal misfortunes. This is important while dating. When you are courting someone, you have to see him or her as apples. Understand that you will always experience some rotten apples in a bunch. It is not realistic to think that the person you are in a relationship with is never going to hurt your feelings. When someone hurts your feelings, it is like biting into a rotten apple and tasting its bitterness. If you choose to stay in an unhealthy relationship, hoping that the taste will change, you will only disappoint yourself. If you start dating someone and he or she turns out to be a rotten apple, stop eating. I can understand the first bite, maybe a second, but a third, fourth and fifth bite, shame on you. So what should you do if you get a bad apple? Try a different apple, until you get a healthy one.

UPDATE YOUR STATUS

Maranda C. : "I love you...but my love can't make you better for me..."– Mar. 5, 2011

Frank: "Well said."

Victoria: "Wow! You took the words out of my mouth."

Brad: "True statement."

When Maranda posted her Facebook status, she had 2,074 FB friends and only four people "liked" her status. Later on that day, she said "Never give away your affections, people don't value what they don't have to work for." Maranda hit the nail directly on the head. Why waste time, energy, and finances on bad apples? Most people do not fully understand what it takes when you sacrifice your time, energy and finances for them. Many simply take it, because it is expected, not because it is appreciated. When you are expected to give, some people will take as much as they can with no regard for your long-term wellness.

FACEBOOK QUOTE

"I want to kiss a FROG & have my PRINCE CHARMING... Not kiss a FROG & still have the FROG!!! Something's got to give!!!"

Victoria Pickard

Dr. Kevin A. Williams, Biblical scholar and Theologian, said it best while standing in front of a large congregation. "A relationship cost twice the emotions of an education." In other words, take the stress and mental anguish you felt during school and double it. We all have to admit that going to school is much easier than dating or being in an exclusive relationship. Dr. Williams went on to talk about how so many people exhaust time on a "feel good emotion", and many never stopped to think about what they could have accomplished during that wasted time. Among the congregation, he asked some to be courageous and tell him the longest they have been in an unmarried relationship. Some said three years. Others said five, nine, and the longest of about 16 years. I observed as some chuckled and made fun, but what are some of the areas of your life you have wasted time, energy and finances.

I often tell people, the time you spent trying to make that unhealthy relationship work, you could have graduated with a college degree, let us not mention the money you spent, perhaps a down payment on a house, and what about the energy you put into trying to make it work? Why continue in abuse, sleepless nights, and the division that unhealthy relationships stir up among family and friends? Is that kind of relationship worth it? For some of you, the relationship may be worth the sacrifice. You may believe they are worth the investment. If you know you have a rotten apple and you eat on it anyway, then you deserve the sickness that will come from it. Do not settle, not even for love. The love you have for another person cannot keep you safe from his or her negative behavior. To continue in an unhealthy relationship makes you no different from a battered woman who keeps going back to her abuser. You determine when enough is enough, but until you make that decision, you will continue to get the same results.

CHAPTER 32

STICK TO THE GAME PLAN

IF I DON'T, THEN SOMEBODY ELSE WILL

For her honeymoon night, Caitlyn dreamed of her first time being in a lovely Five Star Hotel, candlelit room, romantic music in the background, champagne and rose petals laid across the bed. Instead, it was in a dorm room during her freshman year of college, lasting a minuscule six minutes. She knew because when they started it was 1:37am, and when he finished it was 1:43am. During our interview, she said, "I really didn't feel anything other than the weight and warmth of his body. Afterwards, I felt grimy because he sweat all over me; then, he had the nerve to ask me if it was okay. I said, sure. I totally lied, saying to myself...YOU GAVE IT UP FOR THAT!?!"

If you could go back, what would you change? Caitlyn readjusted herself in her seat, and after taking a moment to think about the question, she replied saying, "I would have waited. I was so scared of losing him to another girl that I just let him do whatever he wanted and of course he still cheated. Once, I got pregnant, and he paid for me to get an abortion. He even gave me a STD, and lied about being with other women. He would come to me sobbing and begging me not to leave and of course I always took him back. I don't know what I was thinking! I thought if I had sex with him he wouldn't want anybody else. I wanted so badly for him to love me. I thought if I did it, I would keep him. I gave him my body and soul, but it wasn't enough. I feel terrible because it was like my soul longed for him, like he was God or something."

Do you think you did anything wrong Caitlyn? Most people blame the other person right away, but Caitlyn accepted full responsibility for her negative decisions. After thinking long and hard about our question, she said, "Yes, I did a lot of things wrong. I tried to use my body to keep him. If I would have waited like I said I would and did what was right, I wouldn't have gotten pregnant or that STD. I could have done better in school and I wouldn't have wasted so much time and money."

Whether male or female, who can relate to Caitlyn's circumstances? Caitlyn's snowball effect of misfortune started with one decision, and that decision was to have sex outside of her convictions and standard. She made an oath to herself. Her oath was to wait until she got married, but as soon as she got to college, she threw it out the window. Regardless of what her reasons were, she still deviated from her original plan. When you digress from your vision, there can be no success, unless you get back on track. Getting back on track for some may be going back to school, moving back in with your parents, or going to church. Whatever getting back on track is for you, it must be done in order for you to have success in your life. If a man or woman steps out on you because you are not willing to "give it up", I say, screw them. They are the shallow one, not you.

"There are no biceps, triceps, butt or breast that should be able to distract you..."

Dr. Kevin A. Williams

Like many of us, Caitlyn had a vision, but she allowed herself to get distracted. When she became preoccupied outside of that vision, things started to fall apart. She became less focused on her responsibilities and more centered on what she wanted at the time. Caitlyn sought after things that were outside of its time. She tried to force something that was projected for her future into her present. This was four years ago. Now, Caitlyn is 28 years old, engaged to a man she calls her Stallion. Their wedding is five months from her interview. We were fortunate to come across Caitlyn. We believe that Caitlyn's story can be an encouragement for someone in their time of misfortune. But it also serves as a warning for one who chooses to go outside of his or her original plan.

CHAPTER 33
ADVERSE DATERS

Have you ever known or involved yourself with a person who was or is unwilling to commit to a monogamous relationship with you? They say things like, "I'm not ready for a relationship or that's not what I want right now". That same person saying they are not ready for a relationship is the same person engaging in everything that a monogamous relationship entails (i.e. constant communication, erotic/intimate comments and behavior, and sexual activity). I call these people adverse daters. Men are more likely to adopt the role of an adverse dater than women. Women are quicker to commit to monogamy and a long-term relationship. An adverse dater can easily slip into the realm of a Player, because the nature of both characters resemble one another significantly.

Shamilah from Great Brittain recently went through a major break up. Her ten-minute interview turned into 25 minutes. Shamilah had recently been involved with a guy for two years, while pursuing her undergraduate degree at Bennett College. "I met John my second year at Bennett. We started spending most of our free time together, and if we couldn't be together, he would call. I didn't mind because I really liked him. After a while, I guess he noticed I was getting a little anxious about being exclusive. He started telling me he wasn't ready for a relationship because of some things that happened in a previous one. Of course I responded with understanding, but after about three months of dating we started having sex. After about a year, I asked him about being together exclusively, but he would always tell me that he wasn't ready. Like always I would respond with understanding, until finally I got fed up with his bollocks (nonsense).

Why would you call what he was doing nonsense? Wasn't he just being honest with you about his feelings toward monogamy? "I understand he was being 'honest', but when you tell a person you don't want to be together, but you are constantly calling them, spending time with them, their family, and you are having sex with them, that can be confusing to the other person. That's how it was for me. Every time I thought he was over his issues and we were going to progress to the next stage, he would slam the door in my face. I got sick and tired of his games, so I stopped talking to him."

In school, we use to play a game called, "Red Light, Green Light". At the start of the game, everyone forms a line about 20 feet away from the main character (MC). In this game, the MC turns away from the people and says "green light!" At this point, everyone is allowed to move as fast as they can toward the MC to touch him/her. At any point, the MC may say "red light", then turn toward the group. If the MC catches anyone moving, the MC has the right to tell those individuals to start back at the beginning. This is what occurs in adverse dating relationships. One person is always thinking they are progressing in the relationship, only to be told to start over.

A person can get the reputation of being a Player, but they are simply adverse toward monogamy. Being an adverse dater is not a negative thing. By definition, an adverse dater is simply a person who is unwilling; reluctant; disinclined or unenthusiastic about committing to a monogamous relationship. People become adverse daters for a few reasons: They want to be able to focus on their main priorities, they have had previous relationship hurts, or they want to play the field.

Let's discuss the opposite end of the spectrum. For those of you involved with people, you recognize to be adverse toward monogamy. Understand that you are accountable for your knowledge. Stop willfully getting trapped in this web of naiveté? How long did John tell Shamilah that he was not willing to be in an exclusive relationship? Based on my calculations, it was at least over a year. Shamilah stayed within a relationship dynamic where the individual laid it all out on the table, but she chose to stand on a personal conviction, believing that eventually she could change his nature. She should have recognized that he was just using her. Regardless how angry or victimized Shamilah feels, by no means has she been taken advantage of. During Shamilah's interview, she said that she understood John was being honest with her. It is not healthy for one to pursue a relationship with a person who has communicated that they are not ready for a full commitment. The key words here are "full commitment".

DATING VIOLATION #25

If you are practicing abstinence, but the person you're dating has sex with someone else, run for the hills. He or she may want to be with you; but, their commitment level just isn't there. Don't make it your priority to help them be faithful or be a better person, that's their responsibility. The best thing you can do is move on, progression into a relationship will likely result in you getting cheated on.

In this circumstance, Shamilah had no control over John's choice, but she had all the power concerning how she progressed in a relationship with him. If I could have said one thing to Shamilah after her interview, it would have been to tell her to make sure that she looks after herself first. Take responsibility for yourself before you try to nurture and persuade another to commit to you. Occasionally look in the mirror, remind yourself that you are Number One.

CHAPTER 34
FATAL ATTRACTION

The film "Fatal Attraction" was a hit, becoming the second highest grossing film of 1987 starring Michael Douglas, Glenn Close and Anne Archer. The plot was about Dan's one night stand coming back to haunt him when his lover Alex began to stalk him. Although it was understood that their encounter was a simple fling, she became very clingy. At a point in the movie, Dan tells Alex that he had to go back home. As a result, she cuts her wrists. He helps her bandage them, and later leaves. He thinks the affair is forgotten, but she shows up at various places to see him. She waits at his office one day to apologize and invite him to the opera "Madama Butterfly", but he declines. She continually called his office, until he told his secretary not to take any more of her calls. She then called his house at all hours, later she confronts him saying that she was pregnant and planned to keep the baby. Although he wanted nothing to do with her, she argued that he must take responsibility. Dan even moved to another city, but Alex found him there. The lead female (Alex) in the film has been discussed by psychiatrists and has been used as an illustration for a mental condition called Borderline Personality Disorder (BPD). The disorder typically involves unusual levels of instability in mood, interpersonal relationships, self-image, identity, and behavior. BPD disturbances also may include self-harm. Without treatment, symptoms may worsen, leading (in severe cases) to suicide attempts. Individuals with BPD can be very sensitive to the way others treat them, reacting strongly to criticism. Their feelings toward others often change from positive to negative, usually after a seeming threat of losing someone or disappointment. Impulsive behaviors are common, including alcohol or drug abuse, unsafe sex, and reckless behavior in general. So, when does

143

an attraction become fatal? An attraction becomes fatal when you become enslaved to a habit, practice, something or someone that brings about severe psychological or physical trauma.

WHITNEY HOUSTON

Ms. Houston was honored with numerous awards and accolades recognizing her worldwide success through the music and movie industries. With total career awards in excess of 400, she was recognized as the most awarded female artist of all time. She held the respect and esteem of millions. Despite all of her strengths and abilities, she had fatal attractions, things that gripped her so incredibly strong and enslaved her to deadly pleasures. The realities of Ms. Houston's marriage to Bobby Brown surfaced in 2003 when police responded to a domestic violence call from her about her husband. They found her with a cut lip and bruised cheek. Their marriage was further revealed in Bravo's 2005 reality show "Being Bobby Brown," which showed both Ms. Houston and Bobby Brown in unbelievably compromising circumstances. Accompanied by rumors of drug use, in 2002, Ms. Houston sat down for an interview with ABC News, Diane Sawyer. She referred casually to having used cocaine and marijuana, but drew the line at crack in what turned into a well known cliché:

"First of all, let's get one thing straight," she told Sawyer. "Crack is cheap. I make too much money to ever smoke crack. Let's get that straight. OK? We don't do crack. We don't do that. Crack is whack."

This was her mindset at the time, speaking as if any other illegal drug use is any more acceptable. Her attraction to something that wasn't good for her was her primary influence, teacher and master. Fans were stricken with disbelief as they watched her deteriorate. What happened to the beautiful, classy, well spoken woman many knew and admired?

Furthermore, in 2009, Ms. Houston talked to Oprah Winfrey about her marriage to Bobby Brown, saying that there was physical abuse on both sides, and marijuana laced with cocaine was her drug of choice during their time together. While she declared herself drug free, she returned to rehab in 2011.

Although she was no longer with Bobby Brown, the lasting effects of that relationship were obvious. Some connections are so strong, so penetrating that it takes years of cleaning up before one is able to walk confidently and strong again. Ms. Houston seemed to be on her way toward a powerful comeback by making new and positive connections with people like Kim Burrell. Considering her life, we can conclude that despite her intelligence, strength, classiness, success or eloquence, there is always something or someone that can bring you down.

OTHER FATAL ATTRACTIONS

On May 28, 1992 The New York Times published an article about a teacher being found guilty for murder in White Plains, N.Y. Carolyn Warmus was convicted of killing her lover's wife in the second trial of the case that came to be known nationally as the "Fatal Attraction" murder. In its seventh day of deliberations, the jury sent a note that it had reached a decision at 11:17 a.m. Wednesday; and, within twenty minutes, a court officer was snapping handcuffs on Warmus, a former Westchester County teacher portrayed by prosecutors as obsessed with a married man she had described to friends as "perfect."

Consider the trial in Brussels, Belgium about the skydiver that died as her final moments were captured by the video camera on her helmet?

A jury found fellow skydiver, Els "Babs" Clottemans, guilty of the murder of friend, Van Doren. The crime was motivated by a deadly rivalry for the affections of Marcel Somers, the lover they shared. Sadly, both women were married. Their obsession for someone, that didn't belong to either of them, resulted in the death of one and a 30-year prison sentence for the other.

What are your fatal attractions? Stalking, being overly dependent, rushed sexually activity, invasion of privacy (i.e. uninvited visitations, reading their messages), manipulating behavior, communicating threats, and being violent or abusive are all signs that you are fatally attracted to something or someone. Why try to be with a person that doesn't want you? Relationships are about how you can mutually benefit one another.

FACEBOOK QUOTE

"Women cry over men, men look dumbfounded for women.......Aye
stupid, there's more. Pick ya face up, where's your self respect?"

Clarence Davidson

Don't be that person who joins a church to get the attention of the Pastor or that person who takes college courses because you're trying to be near someone you like. It is insanity to attempt to occupy space in another person's life, especially if he or she doesn't want you there. Can you move on in a mature manner, if you find out a candidate doesn't want you anymore? You can't make someone love you. I'll say it again. You can't make someone love you. If you could make a person love you, would it really be worth it in the end?

CHAPTER 35
HANDS OFF
"THE ENGAGED & MARRIED"

I was recently informed about a facebook inbox, from a female addressing some unresolved issues from a relationship that happened over 3 years ago:

Initiator: I inbox you because 4 years ago I walked in and saw you having sex with my boyfriend. I haven't been able to fully get over how much it hurt me. It was such a long time ago, but I still have the images in my mind and I'm still dealing with the hurt from that situation…

Respondent: I am so sorry and I truly apologize for what I did to you. I really didn't understand the results my actions would have on myself or anybody else. I have truly changed since then and words cannot express how sorry I am. I regret my actions and how I allowed myself to get involved in something that contributed to your hurt. I have asked God for forgiveness and from the bottom of my heart I ask for your forgiveness.

Initiator: Thanks for being honest and admitting your part in that situation. I also appreciate you acknowledging how you were then vs. now. I forgive you…

This happens every day, and not all circumstances end as smoothly. Some people cannot or will not move on from those feelings of hurt with a simple apology. As a result of her positive response, the Initiator was able to achieve a level of closure and extend forgiveness. Instead of responding with humility and remorse, some people would have responded negatively. I have heard people say things like, "Well, they were cheating with other people too." People fail to realize that you are responsible for your actions, even if someone else is involved. Not taking responsibility, having an unremorseful heart, or playing the blame game exhibits immense immaturity.

RESPECT THE GAME

As a Single person, I encourage you not to get involved with the Betrothed or Married. There must be honor in the game, which leads me to Dating Violation #16. Listed below are various relationship types you should never romantically involve yourself in for any reason:

- Mono-Dating relationships
- Poly-Dating relationships
- Engaged
- Married

Anyone knowingly involved with people in any of these relationship categories are committing Adultery, which is a major Dating violation. Socially it may be common practice, but at some point, you are going to want an unadulterated relationship. Consider what you are sowing, what you do to others will come back on you. It is called the Law of Reciprocity: for every action, there is an equal and opposite result. It is a fixed principle built into creation. The apostolic priest Paul said, "Whatever a person sows that will he also reap." Essentially, this means that every action has a predictable consequence according to Don Rousu. He goes on to say, "If I sow corn, I'll get corn, not potatoes. If I sow radishes, I'll get radishes, not squash. If I sow beans, I'll get beans, not watermelons."

A tree that is planted does not grow overnight, it takes decades to mature. In life, when you do things you know are not good, you are planting seeds. Sometimes things can start off innocent, but over time those seeds start to take root and those roots spread out over the land of your emotions. Before you know it, you are trapped with something you seemingly cannot get rid of.

My Grandmother decided that she wanted to do certain landscaping. Her plan was to have a particular tree removed out of her yard. She wanted to remove this tree because it attracted various animals and dripped Sap on our cars. Prior to making arrangements for the tree to be removed, the landscaper came to my Grandmother and said, "Your tree is very healthy and mature. Unfortunately, roots can grow as long as several times the length of the branches in any direction. If I were to uproot the tree, I risk damaging residential underground plumbing. Since there are no apparent hazards created by the roots, I recommend simply cutting the tree down and grinding the stump. This will ultimately impede root growth. I recommend Stump removal because Stumps are sometimes able to regenerate into new trees."

My Grandmother never fully got rid of the entire tree; its roots are embedded within her land. When you involve yourself with someone who is already spoken for, you pollute yourself and the roots of adultery take over your life. Cosmetically you may look fine after cutting it down, but now it's got roots in you so deep, you'll never truly get rid of its side effects. The shame and dishonor will last forever, and those who know will never forget.

REALITY CHECK QUIZ

Let's say you have become romantically involved, which is often the case when spending a lot of time with someone. Of course, sometimes things just happen, and maybe you didn't know they were dating someone else or married. You must immediately disconnect and don't give it a moment's thought. Unremorsefully, I have knowledge of some who have said, "Well, I didn't know about you", to the spouse of the person they were having sex with. Ignorance is not justification. Your unawareness doesn't relieve you from responsibility in such matters.

SO THE REALITY CHECK QUESTION IS:

Am I willing to do what is right for me and others, not limited to disconnecting from someone who is already involved with someone else?

Yes _____   No_____

If your answer is No, consider this fact. If a person is romantically involved with you and someone else, then that person already has an unfaithful character. You may say, "Well they can change." They can change, but you don't have the power to change them, and why would you want someone like that? If a person cheated and left their significant other for you, it's only a matter of time before they cheat on you. If you are the person that settles for a one night stand or is content with being the "Booty Call", search your heart. Is that who you want to be? Is that the legacy you want to leave? At the end of the day, is it something you can be proud of?

BREAKING NEWS

Today I was informed about a very peculiar murder suicide two days ago in the Greensboro, North Carolina area. I used the term peculiar because cases like that are not common in that area. According to an article entitled "Messy Love Triangle" by Margaret Moffett Banks, John Newsom and Dioni L. Wise, staff writers of the Greensboro, North Carolina, News & Record. Mary Ann Holder shot five children, two of her own, her former lover Randy Lamb and then killed herself. Two of the children died and three were in critical condition. The article went on to say, "This much is clear: Mary Ann Holder and Randy Lamb had an affair. Accusations and restraining orders followed. Naked pictures sent via text, stalking, threats of a civil suit and worse. Lamb's wife, Jennifer Swann Lamb, claimed Holder followed her, tried to run her off the road, even switched her son's school to the one attended by the Lamb's son. Most other facts paint a murkier picture of what led Holder on Sunday to shoot Randy Lamb in the arm, killed her two sons and niece, and then committed suicide not before critically wounding three other children who later died at the hospital.

According to digtriad.com, Deputies first got word of Lamb's injury in a 911 call at 9:08 a.m. Lamb's wife called 911 after her husband told her he had been shot near the GTCC Aviation Center. Investigators believe Holder shot Lamb around 8:52 a.m. Sheriff Barnes said that Lamb and Holder had at one time been in an affair that ended in what appears to be a bitter breakup. Court documents show that Holder filed restraining orders against Lamb and his wife, saying they stalked and harassed her and that Lamb constantly drove past her house. Lamb's wife filed a restraining order against Holder, saying she would constantly call and text their cell phones and that Holder also sent nude pictures. Lamb's wife file an alienation of affection claim, which in North Carolina allows someone who is cheated on to sue the person their spouse had an affair with. After receiving information from Lamb, deputies went to Holder's home on Cocoa Drive in Pleasant Garden to look for the suspect around 9:22 a.m. Around that same time, detectives said Holder arranged to pick up her son Zach at a location where he had been spending the night. At 10:11 a.m., a deputy spotted Holder's car on Remora Road. When he turned to approach the car, he saw a "puff of smoke" and believed the suspect shot herself at that time. The deputy found Mary Ann Holder dead in the car. They also found Zachary Smith shot in the head in the backseat. Investigators then went to Holder's house on Cocoa Drive, where they found Dylan Smith dead. Sheriff Barnes said that Holder left behind a note in which she took responsibility for the shootings and apologized for her actions. He also said the note implied that she had been "wronged" in some way, and she was angry with how the relationship with Lamb ended. "We may never know exactly what her thoughts were and why," said Sheriff Barnes.

The question that many of us had was, "Why?" As relevant as that question is I believe we should primarily consider how it could have been avoided. Not all illegitimate romantic affairs end in such tragedy, but they all have the potential to escalate. Typically we stand in judgment of others in such cases, but I believe everyone can learn a valuable lesson from this tragic circumstance. I ask you to reflect back when you were in a stressful, worrisome, fearful, and dejecting or neglectful relationship. Many people are one circumstance from having a nervous breakdown or reacting violently, but if we follow appropriate principals, we can avoid such misfortunes.

LEGAL RISK FACTOR

There are legal risk for getting romantically involved with a married person. In a few states, civil suits can be brought against the cheating party. According to myfamilylaw.com, the spouse who was cheated on – the "injured" spouse – can, in a few states, still bring legal action against the cheating party for "alienation of affection", also known as "Heart Balm Torts," "Revenge," or "Spousal Theft". Alienation of Affection(s) is known as a legal action charging someone with the intentional and malicious interference with a Stage III relationship (marriage). Typically this occurs when one spouse has been cheating on by the other and is caught. There is another similar legal claim related to extramarital sex called "Criminal Conversation", which has slightly different elements.

Criminal conversation is the name for a civil (not criminal, as the name implies) lawsuit requiring the plaintiff to declare and prove the incident of sexual intercourse (adultery) between the defendant (3rd party) and the plaintiff's spouse. Many single people think that if the person is separated from their spouse it's ok, but it's not (even a temporary separation will not be a defense). Not even if the plaintiff gave their spouse permission to have intercourse with the defendant. Though the two are very similar, an action for "Alienation of Affection" does not require proof of extramarital sex (opening the door to suits against those who engaged in an "emotional affair" or those who otherwise encouraged the demise of a marriage).

In cases of "Alienation of Affection" lawsuits, a plaintiff simply has to prove that:

- Love at some point existed within the marriage.
- Love between the married couple was destroyed (or "alienated").
- A third party's malicious conduct contributed to or caused the loss of affection.

REALITY CHECK QUIZ

Who lost the most? Clearly it was Mary Anne Holder and her family. Undoubtedly her involvement with a married man contributed to her irrational behavior, and decisions and it obviously put her in some legal trouble. Unfortunately, innocent children died all because of the selfish, disrespectful actions of two people. I dare not blame her for all of the misfortune that transpired between both families, but let's be realistic. If Mary Anne Holder possessed some of the core values discussed in this book, could this have likely been avoided? Hopefully you've noticed by now that I have primarily addressed the conduct of Mary Anne Holder and not the cheating husband. This book is for people who are single, not for those who are married. When people get married, I call them "Retirees" because marriage is a public declaration that those two people are officially out of the game. As a single person, you must be respectful when couples are having trouble in their marriage. It is not your responsibility, nor do you have the right to come in and be the void filler. Whether you're their friend or not, if a person is having difficulties in their marriage, redirect them toward their spouse, encouraging them to work it out. Once you've done that keep a safe distance.

SO THE REALITY CHECK QUESTION IS:

Are my wants so important that I am willing to destroy another person's relationship or marriage?

Yes _____ No_____

If your answer is 'Yes' then the content in this book, presently may not be very helpful to you. Those who willingly commit adultery to procure a mate have likely developed an unrealistic outlook. Examples might include:

- If he or she leaves their spouse, we can be together happily ever after
- I won't get caught
- he or she loves me more than their spouse
- he or she will be better off with me, we are kindred spirits, we are friends

These are all delusions; false beliefs held with absolute conviction despite superior evidence. Don't be stupid. In Mary Anne's case, all the evidence was there. The real problem arose when Mary Anne broke the rules of Dating. As stated before, the rules protect you. She violated the code of ethics when she decided to tantalize or accept the advances of a married man. Maybe it started off innocent, with the Husband sharing his marital problems. Naturally, you want to help, but at some point sirens go off and warning lights start to flash saying run. Don't miss the warning signs of mischief. If Mary Anne would have known her worth, she would have also known the worth of those she hurt and could have prevented such tragedy. How can you see the worth in others if you cannot see it in yourself? In honor of those lost and hurt in that horrific circumstance, I say to you, learn your worth.

Chapter 36
From Companionship to Engagement

At some point, you are not just going to be a candidate anymore. People close to you may make rapid shifts from companionship to engagement, but as we have discussed, you must take it slow.

"Being single can offer a unique advantage in the pursuit of good relationships. You have the opportunity to step back, take an inventory, learn and grow, and be far more ready for a healthy relationship. Instead of leaping headlong into the next romance, slow down and make some personal discoveries that will increase your chances of having your future relationships be more successful."

Nina Atwood

Some date a couple of months, then move rapidly through the relationship stages, but it is not a race. Other people take years to go from one relationship stage to the next. Do what is best for you. Remember, what works for others may not work for you. Let's make two things very clear: Engagement is on an entirely different level because much more commitment, time, attention and sacrifice are required, but engagement is only a step up from dating. Get out of the mindset of thinking of dating and engagement as permanent. As easy as you got in, is as easy as you can get out.

Section IV
Reality Check

When our eyes and heart deceive us, that's when we need a Reality Check. This section gives sound advice for both genders, providing information and direction to resources that can help you improve yourself and competently evaluate the quality of other candidates. This section will also help you remove the scales from your eyes concurrently revealing personal power. Our emotions are necessary, but we must use our brains when dating. Decisions should be based on logic and facts, not one's emotions.

"Transmit it logically by confronting reality, formulating strategy, accepting responsibility, celebrating victory and learning from defeat."

Dr. John C. Maxwell

CHAPTER 37
DATING VIOLENCE

Every nine seconds, in the United States, a woman is assaulted or beaten. Statistically, domestic violence is the leading cause of injury to women—more than car accidents, muggings, and rapes combined. Nearly one in five teenage girls who have been in a relationship said that a boyfriend threatened violence or self-harm, if presented with a breakup. Everyday in the United States, more than three women are murdered by their boyfriends. Domestic violence victims lose nearly eight million days of paid work per year in the US alone—the equivalent of 32,000 full-time jobs. Based on reports from ten countries, between fifty-five percent and ninety-five percent of women who had been physically abused by their partners had never contacted non-governmental organizations, shelters, or the police for help.

Some dating basics, according to Loveisrespect.org, teach that relationships exist on a spectrum, from healthy to unhealthy to abusive. A healthy relationship exhibits traits of honesty, respect for individuality and respect of boundaries. Indications that a relationship is unhealthy are actions like:

- Intense jealousy and insecurity
- Checking your cell phone, social accounts and/or emails without permission
- Frequent mood swings
- Isolating you from family or friends
- False accusations
- Overly possessiveness
- Volatile rage

When someone sexually assaults you or treats you in a harmful, injurious, or offensive way, they have abused you. There are many forms of abuse, but they are not all considered violent. Violence is a swift and intense, rough or injurious physical force, action, or treatment. The goal of violence is to damage through bodily distortion. Of course, a man should never put his hands on a woman to harm her. Women also have a moral obligation not to provoke men and must avoid violence at all cost.

They say the best way to a man's heart is through his stomach, but that is not true. The way to a man's heart is through gentleness. Culturally, men are taught to be exteriorly firm and tough because rigidity is associated to masculinity. Men that appear too gentle may be seen as weak, pathetic, or sensitive, so they overcompensate in certain areas when their masculinity is questioned. This could be the reason why most men refrain from showing certain emotions in public or resist excessive public affection. Since most men associate gentleness to femininity, they expect women to handle them with kindness and calmness. When a man observes a woman demonstrating masculine toughness his mentality shifts. In his mind, he is not dealing with the spirit of a woman, but that of another man. He no longer views the woman as feminine but masculine, and masculinity is associated with manhood. Some times men deal with other men rigidly, harshly or toughly. To women that do not understand the culture of masculinity, the way a man deals with another man may come across as insensitive or harsh.

If you don't want a man hitting on you, then never put your hands on a man. During the Chris Brown & Rihanna incident, I listened intently to Rihanna's every word during her interview on ABC with Diane Sawyer. I listen for what women won't admit or say outright in domestic violence cases. She said something that most people overlooked. She said, "Even if

I hit him first, that makes it okay for him to do that to me?" A comment like that shows signs of a double standard. It insinuates that it is more acceptable for a woman to hit a man. Rihanna's comment intimates she believed, if she hit Brown, it would have been more acceptable than if Brown hit her. Socially, that may be the case, but legally, it is not. Being a woman never gives you the right to put your hands on a man.

Males are taught, from a young age, to never hit females. When a little boy and girl get into a fight during recess at school, the boy is immediately told that he is not supposed to hit girls. Little girls, on the other hand, are rarely taught the same, so they grow up thinking that it is acceptable to provoke masculinity. When someone puts their hands on you to harm you, what are your first thoughts? Your first thoughts are either flee or defend and fight back. Men are no different, even when the aggression is coming from a woman. To a man, women are supposed to be gentle. A man never expects for a woman to use abusive techniques or deal with him in a masculine manner. Remember, men don't see femininity if a woman is being aggressive and abusive, he sees another man and his innate drive to conquer clashes with his intellect. When a woman continually provokes a man and puts pressure on him, she becomes like a fly at an outdoor cookout. Before you know it, he has done something inappropriate, while trying to defuse the situation and keep his manhood intact.

Rihanna said she and Brown were in the car after the Grammys, and he was driving. Over the next thirty minutes, this is what happened: She saw a text message on his cell phone from an old girlfriend and she got angry. "I caught him in a lie, and he wouldn't, he wouldn't tell the truth. So, I wouldn't drop it. I wouldn't drop it. I kept saying… I couldn't take that he kept lying to me, and he couldn't take that I wouldn't drop it."

The truth of the matter is if Brown wanted Rihanna to drop the situation or discuss it at a later time, she should have done it. Instead, she admitted that she wouldn't drop it. I have no doubt that Rihanna provoked Brown on some level, NOT to make him so angry that he would harm her; it was likely an attempt to force him to do what she wanted, which was talk about the situation, and unfortunately it escalated further. If that was the case, like many others, I find fault on her end as well.

Men, women have no right to hit you and you have no right to hit them. When a man becomes abusive, his acts supersede the ill characteristics of the woman. Now, nobody cares if she poked you in the forehead. She may have followed you, hitting you in the back and on the head as you walked away, but it doesn't matter anymore. The fact that you hit her in an abusive manner overrides everything she did prior to your offenses.

Men are generally bigger and stronger than women; so, it is not an unreasonable expectation to maintain self control, and refrain from abusing a woman. Domestic violence will always remain as long as people lack discipline within communicating properly. Instead, we yell and become aggressive, but we expect to get a positive response. As a man, what should I do if I'm trying to deescalate the situation, but she won't back down?

1. REMOVE YOURSELF

Touch her only with the purpose of getting her off of you. Sometimes going to another room is not enough, or walking away is not enough, especially if you're dealing with a very aggressive and ill-tempered female. Lower your pride and if you have to run, then run. Don't look at running as a cowardly act or like she won. Look at it as if you are taking every measure to remove yourself from the situation. On the other hand, if she wants to leave, then let her leave.

2. CALL LAW ENFORCEMENT

Many times calling law enforcement is the best protection from accusations of domestic violence. It speaks volumes that you are taking the necessary steps to avoid violence and want to do what is right. Trust me. An enraged woman will not hesitate to call the cops on you, even if you haven't harmed her. It is not until later, they realize they overreacted.

My words are not meant to be offensive to either gender or appear as though I am siding with one gender over another. My hope is that I encourage accountability from both men and women. Of course, I would NEVER make any excuse for a man who physically abuses a woman. A man who abuses a woman, needs a good beating himself; but, it is not right for woman to think it is more acceptable to be abusive toward men. Physical harm, aggression and undue pressure from a woman will often create internal turmoil for a man. Men use force to deal with most conflicts. They are this way because the culture of masculintiy is much different than the culture of femininity.

My preference is that all women remain lady-like, for men to be gentlemen, and talk through conflicts, rather than behaving inappropriately. Never slap, poke, push, pull or follow a man trying to get your points across. If he leaves, it's because he needs to leave. Let him go and come as he pleases; a man handles confrontation differently than a woman. On the other hand, a man should never grab, jerk, or push a woman because he's angry or she isn't doing what he wants her to do. Understand that if she is angry or has a concern, she is going to want to discuss it.

Learn when to discuss matters at a later time, when the both of you are calm and can be rational. A good rule of thumb when dealing with conflict is to:

1. Never discuss the issue when either of you are irritated. Cool off. Try not to engage the situation angry.

2. View the circumstance objectively; try to view each conflict as if you are a third party to the situation.

3. Work to collaborate; seek to achieve a win-win solution. Have a no loser's mentality, where everybody wins.

In review, women want gentle-men and men never want aggression from women, rather gentleness, kindness, and calmness. Even if the man has done something wrong, it is better for the woman to be gentle with her touch and tone. Every day, when men are out with the boys, or at work, they are expected to be a certain way. When your man is around you, he needs to know that he can just be himself. That's how you get to the heart of a man.

If you are being abused contact the National Domestic Violence Hotline at www.thehotline.org.

(800) 799-SAFE (7233)

Or

TTY (800) 787-3224

CHAPTER 38
QUALITY

"The quality of a person's life is in direct proportion to their commitment to excellence; regardless of their chosen field of endeavor…the difference between a successful person and others is not a lack of strength, not a lack of knowledge, but rather in a lack of will."

Vince Lombardi

Have you ever considered the star ratings of hotels? Of course you have. While traveling, who doesn't want to stay in a Five Star hotel? Star rating systems are intended to serve as guidelines for guests who are making hotel reservations. The rating or standard of a hotel is often influenced by their food services, entertainment, view, room size, fitness centers, spas, location and additional amenities. If you are finicky about the quality of hotels you stay in, why are you not as particular about the people you date? When we have the option of selection or acceptance, it is vital that the candidate we choose be one that possesses good qualities.

Often, we get into relationships with blinders on, almost as if we don't want to know the truth in the beginning. Unfortunately, by the time we're ready to accept the truth about people, it's often too late. The damage has already been done. I know dozens of women who now have babies with unsupportive fathers and others who have co-signed on property with unreliable significant others. If those same individuals were diligent in determining the quality of those they were in a relationship with, they could have saved themselves a huge heartache.

Within each individual there lies a power or an ability simply to choose who will or will not be in their lives. Imagine how many people have come into and gone out of your life, but have made emotional withdrawals and/or caused some damage. Most of the time, I hear blame towards the other person for the hurt in his or her life, but understand that you have the power to accept or deny him or her access. Today is a day for change, and you will no longer allow just anybody in your life. You will investigate, learn about him or her and determine if he or she is worthy of your time.

The reality of dating is parallel to a job interview. When we are going for employment, we sit in front of an interviewer while he or she gathers information about us. An interviewer will ask us challenging questions, and we try our best to convince him or her that we are the best fit or most suitable for the position. When you are dating, you are interviewing for a place in that individual's life as he or she is interviewing for a place in yours. Do not feel that it is unethical to be open or ask challenging questions to get to know him or her. This is not to say that you lay your cards on the table all at once. There has to be a level of transparency, each candidate should understand the potential quality of life that he or she might have with you. Additionally, don't be afraid to interview his or her parents and inner circle about his or her personality, to some extent. Ask questions about, how he or she treats his or her parents and/or guardians, how he or she did in school, or his or her work ethic. Remember, you are not looking for the right package (i.e. your laundry list) but a suitable package. The suitable package is the person that you believe will add to your life, not fulfill all of your wildest fantasies. Looking for what is suitable, instead of holding each candidate to a laundry list of standards, exhibits maturity.

CHAPTER 39
LADIES

Ladies, a sure way to scare off a good candidate is by comparing yourself to him. Boasting about your possessions, accomplishments and how he should come up to your level is an unacceptable practice. A man never sees this advance as a reasonable challenge for him to "step his game up." If you express yourself in such a manner, he will likely view you as arrogant, egotistical, conceited, and superficial. I'm not saying that you should lower your standards, but never put a man down. If a candidate is not what you think he should be, move on to the next candidate. In response to this subject, a colleague told me, "It sounds like you're telling women that they should just accept anything from men or just any kind of man. If that man is not up to par, is it not more appropriate to push him to be better?" "Absolutely", I replied. "Women must maintain their standards without fail, but they also have to be realistic. For example, if a man is unemployed and not actively looking for a job, or he is content working a dead end job, it's very simple, don't date him!"

Let's say, you like a guy who is pursuing you and you want to date him. Be willing to accept who he is and do not expect him to change overnight. If you are on top of your game, wait for that man to step his game up before you let him date you. On the other hand, be open to the reality that he may never change, especially, if it is how he was when you met him. If you involve yourself with a man that is jobless, has children and has no prospects, remember you chose him. No one put a gun to your head and said, "You are going to be with this person." Just because you see potential does not mean he is good for you.

"Seen potential is not manifested potential. Potential must be stimulated, and once stimulated, it must be demonstrated."

#DRBRIGGS

Ladies, if you want to help bring the potential you see out of a man, be willing to sacrifice the time, energy and finances that it requires. If not, wait for him to improve himself or move on.

GENTLEMEN STILL EXIST

Believe it or not, chivalry within men still exists. All men enjoy opening doors or running through the rain to get the umbrella. The Gentleman is refortified in him when he completes those minute courtesies for you; he also gains a sense of additional usefulness in your life. It is not uncommon to see younger women opening their own doors. But if they see another man opening the door for his woman, they criticize their man, saying, he's not a gentleman. Ladies, don't blame the man; blame yourself. The reason he doesn't open doors for you is because you don't make him responsible for opening doors for you. Ladies, if you want that man to open doors regularly, then encourage this behavior habitually.

Unfortunately, the character of the modern women can come across as unruly and crude. The mindset of the modern woman is to "rule the world," making men, in a sense, obsolete. Women must be classy, sensible and confident in their identity, but without the tendency to be domineering, leaning towards masculinity. A man can identify what kind of woman you are by observing how you interact with others or on social networks. He can tell if you are easy, unmanageable or sophisticated. He knows when and if he needs to bring his A-game and how long he should wait before he approaches you.

WHAT'S ATTRACTIVE TO MEN?

A Lady who is quiet, but exudes self-confidence is most attractive to men. Deep down, men are not fulfilled by loud, ill-tempered, and excessively opinionated women. When a lady can command respect without nagging, raising her voice or being aggressive, it is a sight for sore eyes to a man.

WHAT REPELS MEN?

Closed minded, negative women repel good men. They know what they know and could care less about what a man thinks. These are your head strong women, usually judgmental toward others. You will often hear them express various dislikes about people and what they are always doing wrong. They are often people pleasers, exhibiting a very enthusiastic persona, but are unparalleled privately. I heard a guy once say, he dislikes when a gal doesn't take care of herself. He believed that a woman that does not take good care of her physical appearance is more prone to be less kept up in other areas.

Ladies, get out of the princess paradigm that says, "DO FOR ME, SO I DON'T HAVE TO DO FOR MYSELF!" Most men don't want to feel obligated to take care of a woman hand and foot, especially if they are only dating. Without hesitation, a gentleman will do the things that are socially expected, if he knows she is willing to do it for herself.

Aggression toward a man is probably the best way to get rid of him. Men absolutely despise disrespect from their women, especially public condescension. "Oftentimes, women just don't get it", said my eternal friend, Marcus Witherspoon. "They don't realize they have venom in them. Because they were envenomed, they try to envenom you." A lot of women have experienced some bad relationships, but when they get someone beneficial, they don't know how to care for that man. She may have been involved with a man that she had to yell at to get her points acknowledged. On the other hand, some men may have been aggressive toward her, now she feels she has to be aggressive. Some men may have habitually disappointed her and now her mindset is Men are dogs and I don't trust them. Some men may have verbally abused her, or she may have been raised by parents who behaved this way.

You finally meet a guy who is none of those things. He's gentle, kind, calm, and says things to build your self-esteem. But you yell at him, treat him like a dog, you're disrespectful, and you won't open up your heart. All you did was take that same venom (bitterness) to the new relationship and you wonder why he's distant. Well, you've become a viper and he's trying not to get bitten.

WHAT TO LOOK FOR IN A MAN

Ladies, it is vital to identify various qualities in a man of significance. He must be a man of integrity, honoring his oaths. An oath is nothing more than a promise. His oaths could be honesty within business deals, paying his bills on time, or respecting others. I have observed women struggle with the concept of stability and how stable a man should be. The stability of a future husband should primarily be within the area of his ability to provide food, shelter and protection. He may not be affluent, but he should be able to supply your basic needs and indulge your desires ever so often. Understand that he will never be your idea of a perfect man because that man does not exist. More importantly, it is your duty to reject any man who approaches you that does not meet your standards. Some men think that you should feel privileged if they approach you. If that man does not have all his "ducks in a row", shoot the rest down.

FACEBOOK QUOTE

"Guy: Kiba, when you gone stop playin and be my girl?
Me: You can't even take care of yourself (LMBO). Are you serious???
You can't do anything for me. YOU don't even have your own car.... Get
outta here LOL"

Shakiba Lisbon

If you are a woman of standard, have an education, good job, home
or business, why would you require anything less from a man? Possess
and exhibit a character and confidence that will make any man want to
get his priorities in order.

WHAT ABOUT THE CONDUCT OF A LADY?

Ladies, even the way you dress must be with discretion and elegance.
Your style of clothing is influenced by your sex drive, mood and what you
are currently trying to attract. If you want a man to see you as a lady, be
mindful about what you wear and how you behave. Since men are visually
perceptive, their initial appreciation of women is based on appearance
and conduct. He then explores the intellectual side of you. If a woman
sexually tantalizes the average male, he'll likely take the bait. After a man
gets a taste, he will likely be less interested in the intellectual side of her.
This frustrates many women, but the quickest way to lose his interest is
to stimulate him physically.

FACEBOOK QUOTE

"If you get a new job, there is a probation period…you won't be able to
get the benefits until you have been on the job faithfully for at least 3-6
months. During that probational time, you have to prove to your job
that you are the right one for the job by coming to work on time, putting

forth effort, etc. So if you have to wait over 90 days to get benefits on your job, then why don't you apply the same strategy to a man? He has to go through a probational period to prove he is worthy of the benefits. Don't give in to easy and too early! Make them wait!!!"

Alexis Alexander

Remember ladies, if you give the physical, you lose the intellectual. I believe this to be true about men because sex is an intoxicant to a man. After he has got a taste, the next time you see each other, he will likely want another taste and another. It never ends.

When you are together, his heart might even "skip a beat" or beat faster. Don't mistake this for love. It's probably the release of dopamine in the pleasure center of the brain. When men are sexually stimulated the neurotransmitters, dopamine, light up areas deep within the brain, triggering feelings of motivation, pleasure, and reward. According to the University of Texas, one of the neurotransmitters playing a major role in addiction is dopamine. Cocaine causes the same affects by flooding your head with dopamine. Dopamine gives you those feelings of giddiness, euphoria, and elation. The dopamine high is additive. It gets us in the mood, and once there's stimulation, it keeps us coming back for more. It occurs in both genders, but I believe it's much more exaggerated in men because of elevated testosterone levels. Instead of his motivation being that of a gentleman trying to get to know a lady as a potential spouse, he'll be looking for her so he can get his next fix.

CHAPTER 40

GENTLEMEN

The reason you are called a Gentleman is because you are expected to be gentle with your lady. It can be confusing because most women express they want a hard, rough and tough man, but they also want a gentle man. They want a man who can step up to the plate and knock the ball clear out of the area, someone who will fight for them and defend them, and they want the gentle man to hold them at night. Be both, the hard man and the gentle man.

I believe that all men are kings, but every man must individually choose what kind of king he will be. Will he be honorable? Will he strive to conduct himself with integrity or behave ignominiously? As a man, you must shift your mentality to determine which woman is qualified to sit with you as queen. Never look for anything that is not equivalent to you. If you have your own home, then set your standard for candidates to have their own home or at least be able to qualify for one. If you have a successful business, then set your standards toward a woman that has her own business or has an entrepreneurial way of thinking. She must be suitable and able to bring something to the table. Don't be egotistical like those who say to women, "Sit back, I'll take care of you." Ninety percent of the time, this approach only creates parasitic, egocentric, hedonistic, and unappreciative princesses. Those men will find themselves stressed and financially depleted before long.

BE DEVOTED TO THE WOMAN

Gentlemen, it is important to be devoted to the woman and not to her external obligations. A man will often observe the needs of a woman and make it his priority to provide and care for her. To devote means to concentrate on a particular quest. This is as serious as devoting time for reading, or devoting your life to God. Devotion to a woman requires one to view her separate from her external responsibilities or compulsions. There is nothing wrong with splurging on or helping a woman, but while in a Stage I relationship, it is important to remind yourself that she can provide for herself. She was doing it before you came along and you should require her to continue. Besides, you're only dating.

Find the woman that is going to help you as you pursue education, debt liberation, or entrepreneurial success. The woman you choose should not be someone that is going to hinder you from accomplishing your goals. She must not be a drama queen. She must be mature and able to handle herself with poise and sophistication. Some men like a little ruffian or toughness in women. If you fancy this sort of woman, then choose one who knows when to turn it on and off. There's nothing more grueling than a woman whose tongue and behavior are unbridled. If you can find a good, wholesome woman that wants to add to you, who will be honest with you and who wants to protect your heart, then you've found a good thing.

SUPERMAN COMPLEX

There are so many women with so many problems and misfortune. As a gentleman, you may feel that intrinsic craving to jump into their pool of problems and rescue them, but you cannot. I identify that innate desire as the "Superman Complex".

Superman had so many unique abilities, such as super strength, lightning speed, laser beams that shot out of his eyes and he could fly. No one ever places emphasis on his super hearing. Superman would be miles away and could still hear the cries of those in trouble. Without his super hearing, Superman would have never been able to respond to people as fast as he did. You will hear the desperation and cries of many troubled women, but understand that you cannot save them all, and you are not Superman. You can only save one, commit to one, belong to one woman. Superman could never commit, belong, or give his whole heart to one person because it was scattered among the masses. He could never belong within a wholesome relationship and fulfill his yearning for normalcy. He was appreciated, esteemed, and treasured by all, but loved by only one whom he could never wholly be with. This was the inevitable sacrifice of his calling.

WHAT TO LOOK FOR (PART I)

The woman you choose must be able to handle who you are and everything that is attached to you. She must appreciate what it took for you to get where you are. A woman that cannot handle where you are or where you are going is equivalent to termites in a beautiful wood frame structure.

I'm asking you to set the standards high for women you encounter. On the other hand, don't require things or qualities that you don't possess yourself. Women want to possess effeminate strength, intelligence and suitability for the man who has chosen them, but they want "Reciprocated Suitability". Reciprocated suitability is the capacity of another to contribute to the other. Don't make too many demands when she is the one making the most sacrifices. She loans you money. She lets you borrow her car because you don't have your own and even pays for dates when you don't have enough for the tab.

To be frank, any reputable woman that continues to court a man in this position for any extended time is probably a keeper. So, step your game up before she realizes she can do better. She may already know she can do better, but because she cares for you, she stays a little longer hoping you will improve. If this is you, share certain visions with her and if possible incorporate her in them. This will enable her to fulfill part of her purpose, which is to help you. When she can see progress, she'll feel more secure about sticking around. When a woman is with a man who was jobless, but he gets a job, she becomes more emotionally secure. She can see progress and can work with that. When that same man gets a promotion or better paying job, her emotional security increases; when she can see stability and consistency, she'll feel even more secure. When she feels this way, she will be able to confidently make a future decision to move further in connection with you. She will believe that you can protect and provide adequately within the role of a man and long-term companion. Work hard, but in working hard, work smart.

"It's important to know that words don't move mountains. Work, exacting work moves mountains."

Danilo Dolci

ENTRAPMENT SCHEMES

We vaguely discussed protecting yourself in previous chapters. I would like to highlight specific areas of protection men should be most alert about. Men are trapped by women in two strategic and effective ways:

1. False Accusations (i.e. rape or physical abuse)
2. Pregnancy Schemes

A false accusation of rape is a false allegation of a forcible sexual assault. Detailed investigations using differing samples and methodologies have found results ranging from 1.5% to 45% of rape accusations being false. The frequency of false rape complaints or other legal authorities is difficult to determine and the absolute value remains unknown.

FBI reports consistently put the number of "unfounded" rape accusations around eight percent. However, "unfounded" is not synonymous with false allegation. Bruce Gross of the Forensic Examiner's said, "This statistic is almost meaningless, as many of the jurisdictions from which the FBI collects data on crime use different definitions of, or criteria for, "unfounded." That is, a report of rape might be classified as unfounded (rather than as forcible rape) if the alleged victim did not try to fight off the suspect, if the alleged perpetrator did not use physical force or a weapon of some sort, if the alleged victim did not sustain any physical injuries, or if the alleged victim and the accused had a prior sexual relationship. Similarly, a report might be deemed unfounded if there is no physical evidence or too many inconsistencies between the accuser's statement and what evidence does exist. As such, some unfounded cases of rape may be false or fabricated, but not all unfounded cases are false."

Another form of terminology used to describe false assault is false accusation of physical abuse. Fathers' Organizations now estimates that up to 80% of domestic violence (DV) allegations against men are false allegations. False or staged DV allegations now appear to be even more frequent in family court cases than false sex abuse allegations, and they are much easier to fabricate according to Fathers' Organizations. With any case of abuse, the man is arrested first and asked questions later; so, in the case of false accusation, it's easy for a man to suffer loss and reputable damage.

What sexually active male hasn't heard these two common statements? "I'm pregnant" or "I might be pregnant." Beware of the woman that will debase herself by attempting to trap you with her vagina or children. She thinks her vagina is gold. If she has a child by you, she feels this will bind you to her or provide her with some sort of monetary security. The latter of this selfish and delusional scheme often works. Now, since we're on the subject about pregnancy schemes, it's only fitting that we also discuss child support for a moment. According to the report mentioned from Custodial Mothers, Fathers and their Child Support by Timothy S. Grall, child support can be ordered by a court in some states until the child is 21 years old or completes college. This report covers parents' own children under 21, rather than applying the Census Bureau's usual definition of children as those under 18 years of age. In 2009, the 5.9 million custodial parents who were due child support under the terms of legal awards or informal agreements were due an annual average of $5,960, or approximately $500 per month. The median amount of child support due in 2009 was $4,450. A total of $35.1 billion in child support payments was due to custodial parents who had agreements for support. The average amount of child support received by custodial parents who were due support payments in 2009 was $3,630, or about $300 per month. Child support can be expensive, especially if you're already living paycheck to paycheck. The average amount of child support received by the 4.2 million custodial parents who received at least some of the support they were due was $5,140, for an average annual income of $32,000. This represented 16.1 percent of their average annual individual income in 2009.

WHAT TO LOOK FOR (PART II)

Unfortunately, many men have a tendency of allowing themselves to be trapped. They allow their affections to bond to a woman before they have analyzed whether or not she is beneficial long term. Many men find themselves in love with women, and sacrificing for them although their connection to them is poisonous to their future. Do not be the typical man that fails to have a criterion of approval for female candidates. As a man, the initial approval of a woman should be her intellect. Although her physical appearance is what initially attracts you to her, it should remain secondary. If you start qualifying women by their intellects and values, you will find less in their package to distract you. A woman's package is her nice smile, her long beautiful hair, her nicely shaped butt, bosom and sophisticated walk. When the standard of her package is inferior to the standard of her mind, you'll be less distracted. The only way to find out what is in the mind of a woman is through consistent and effective communication. Your drive must be to learn as much as you can about her; then, you will be able to determine whether or not she is suitable for your life.

Section V
Dating Violation Glossary

DATING VIOLATION #1

Premarital sexual activity (Not limited to Intercourse, Oral stimulation or Fondling).

Why: Sex complicates Stage I relationships, and clouds proper judgment and decision making. When you give your "goodies" away (male or female), you'll find yourself trying to make a bad relationship work, when ordinarily you would have left during the first signs of trouble.

DATING VIOLATION #2

Stalking: unwanted and obsessive attention by one person to another person. Stalking includes following the victim in person and/or monitoring them. (See Chapter 18)

DATING VIOLATION #3

Physical Violence: It is never appropriate to put your hands on anyone with the intentions to cause them harm, unless you are protecting yourself from being harmed.

DATING VIOLATION #4

Going broke to impress a date is always a bad sign and an indication that you are on your way to a relationship casualty. Lack of finances can cause undue strain on an underdeveloped relationship. As discussed in Chapter Four, make it your goal to achieve financial security and comfort before diving head first into a relationship.

DATING VIOLATION #5

Putting a potential candidate before your children (legal minors) is a major violation. Candidates must show an interest in both you and your child. (See Chapter 5)

DATING VIOLATION #6

Treating a courtship like it's a marriage is a sure way to emotionally trap yourself with a candidate that may not be good for you in the long run. Be patient and give the relationship time to develop properly.

DATING VIOLATION #7

Casual sex affairs are strictly prohibited. It is already a long and arduous process trying to get to know a person and prove whether their trustworthy or not. Why would you add sex into the mix? (See Chapter 29)

DATING VIOLATION #8

Pressuring someone to have sex is strictly prohibited. As someone in control of your life, it is your responsibility not to fall to trickery and games.

DATING VIOLATION #9

Lending Money

Why: Loaning money has the potential to create strain within any relationship type. If you don't have currency exclusively for the purpose of lending, then don't lend it.

Rule of thumb: If you can't afford not to get the money back then don't loan it. The best way to loan money is to know that if you don't get it back, it will have very little affect on your personal economy. (See Chapter 16)

DATING VIOLATION #10

Playing the victim and blaming others for what happened to you in the past is prohibited. People don't have to put up with your ill behavior because you have been hurt by others. Not being able to get over your past is a reason why you should not be dating right now; so take the necessary time to get yourself together. (See Chapter 20)

DATING VIOLATION #11

Putting undo pressure on someone who is not ready to go to the next level is unfair. Give a Stage I relationship time to develop on its own. When it's time to progress to a higher stage, both people will have no doubts. (See Chapter 13)

DATING VIOLATION #12

Threats to break up or attempts to temporarily escape the relationship are prohibited. You are either with that person or you are not, so don't toy with his or her heart. Treat him or her the way you want to be treated. (See Chapter 26)

DATING VIOLATION #13

Putting your business on social networks is discouraged. If you are courting someone else, you also have to consider how your actions affect him or her. (See Chapter 21)

DATING VIOLATION #14

Dating because you are lonely is a sure way to get used and abused. Learn how to be content being alone, learn to love yourself before allowing someone else to enter your love life.

DATING VIOLATION #15

Dating someone for money or sex is strictly prohibited. (See Chapter 29)

DATING VIOLATION #16

Listed below are various relationship types you should never involve yourself in for any reason:

- Mono-Dating relationships
- Poly-Dating relationships
- Engaged
- Married

Anyone knowingly involved with people in any of these relationship categories are committing a major Dating violation. Socially, it may be common practice, but at some point, you are going to want a meaningful relationship yourself. Consider what you are sowing because it will come back on you. (See Chapter 34)

DATING VIOLATION #17

Living together before marriage is discouraged. (See Chapter 30)

DATING VIOLATION #18

Ignoring the warning signs of a bad relationship (See Chapter 31)

DATING VIOLATION #19

Holding on to old gifts from past relationships like clothing, shoes, pictures, cards, love letters, jewelry, etc. is not a good practice. Get rid of anything that reminds you of an Ex, it only keeps you stuck in the past. (See Chapter 23)

DATING VIOLATION #20

Obsessing over someone you cannot have or coveting someone else's spouse (See Chapter 33)

DATING VIOLATION #21

Enticing or making yourself vulnerable to those who are engaged or married is a major offense to the game. Seek your own and do not covet something that belongs to someone else. (See Chapter 34)

DATING VIOLATION #22

Ladies, disrespecting men is prohibited, no matter the situation. The best thing you can do is remove yourself from any compromising situations that will put you in the position to get out of character or act ill-mannered toward a man. (See Chapter 37)

DATING VIOLATION #23

Missing work and/or school to spend time with someone you're dating.

DATING VIOLATION #24

Cheating: to deceive; influence by fraud; violate the rules or regulations. If you're going to be unfaithful to someone, save them the hurt and end the relationship.

DATING VIOLATION #25

Absolutely, under no circumstance should you call back to back unless it is some sort of MEDICAL or FAMILY emergency. If there is a true medical emergency, obviously you should call 911 first.

Why: These actions are typically seen as needy, immature or clingy. When calling someone, the best thing to do is call once. If you don't want to leave a voice message send a text message, then continue on with your day, while you wait patiently for a reply. (See Chapter 18)

DATING VIOLATION #26

If you are practicing abstinence, but the person you're dating has sex with someone else, run for the hills. He or she may want to be with you; but, their commitment level just isn't there. Don't make it your priority to help them be faithful or be a better person, that's their responsibility. The best thing you can do is move on. Progression into a relationship will likely result in you getting cheated on.

DATING VIOLATION #27

Under no circumstances should you ever co-sign for anyone (i.e. car, student loan, etc.), especially if it's someone you're dating. When you co-sign for others, their debt becomes your debt. People need co-signers for two reasons, bad credit or insufficient income. If they default, you are legally and financially liable to make the payments.

COMING SOON!!!

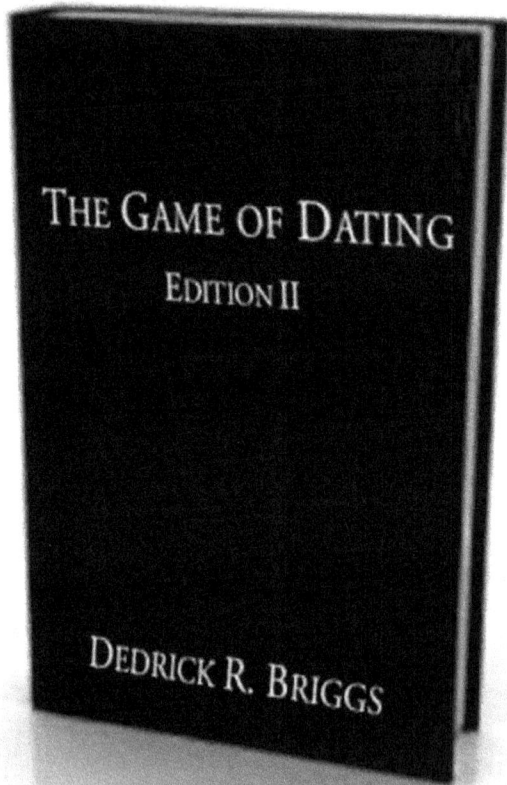

RECOMMENDED SELF HELP BOOKS TO READ:

(audio versions may be available)

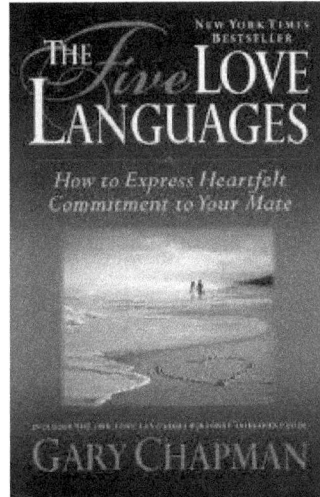

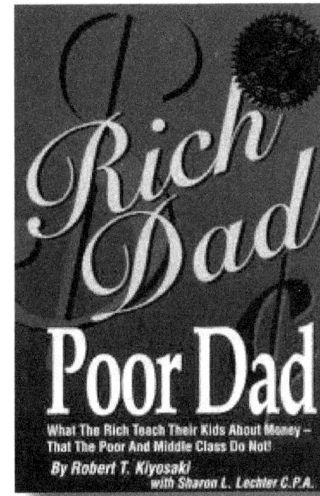

TURNING POINT

REACHING IN ME...

TO FIND ME...

KEVIN A. WILLIAMS

NEW YORK TIMES
BESTSELLER

THE *Five* **LOVE LANGUAGES**

How to Express Heartfelt Commitment to Your Mate

GARY CHAPMAN

THE MILLIONAIRE NEXT DOOR

THE SURPRISING
SECRETS OF
AMERICA'S WEALTHY

READ BY
COTTER SMITH

Thomas J. Stanley, Ph. D.
William D. Danko, Ph. D.

***Rich Dad* Poor Dad**

What The Rich Teach Their Kids About Money –
That The Poor And Middle Class Do Not!

By Robert T. Kiyosaki
with Sharon L. Lechter C.P.A.

"Read, learn, work it up, go to the literature. Information is control."

Joan Didion

Be on the lookout for rising author Juanita Williams. Juanita is a graduate of Bennett College, Greensboro, North Carolina with a Bachelor's degree in Elementary Education. She is currently certified in Elementary Education K-6 and A.I.G. (Academically or Intellectually Gifted). At the beginning of her career as an educator, she worked as a Title I Resource Teacher, which allowed her to work with small groups of students from Kindergarten to Fifth Grade on Reading and Math. She has been called on by a number of colleagues and friends to write letters, biographical sketches, and stories for teacher-constructed tests and to proofread various writings.

Her goal is to become a published author of inspirational, self-help and children's books. She is also currently enrolled in the Children's Literature Institute in her pursuit of becoming a children's author. She is currently working on a manuscript entitled, *"Healing for your Soul"* that involves telling her personal testimony regarding physical healing, accepting what God allows, seeing that as the way He brings you to completeness in Him and gives you an opportunity to bless others.